HEROIC STORIES TO CHANGE YOUR LIFE SERIES

How to Get Out of
THE TRUE SELF TRAP

ALSO BY KALINDA ROSE STEVENSON

Writing Books

Book Writing Made Simple 3-in-1: How to Write a Book the Simple Way
On Writing Words: A Writer's Essential Relations with Words
Writer's Block and Your True Self: 4 Questions to Banish Writer's Block

Book Writing Made Simple Series

Book Writing Made Simple (Volume 1): How to Start Writing a Book with the Right Question
Book Writing Made Simple (Volume 2): How One Question Can Eliminate Your Greatest Obstacle to Writing Your Book
Book Writing Made Simple (Volume 3): Do You Know What Your Reader Really Wants?

Does the Bible Really Say That? Series

Your True Self Identity: How Familiar Translations of Bible Verses in the Gospel of Matthew Hide Your True Identity from You
Gospel of Wealth or Poverty? How Do Bible Verses about Jesus, Wealth, Poverty, and Heaven Affect Your Income?

Kindle Mini Books

Does Positive Thinking Work? When Positive Affirmations Aren't Enough to Change Your Life
The Hidden Reason Why You Are Stuck: A True Story about the Difference between Success and Failure

HEROIC STORIES TO CHANGE YOUR LIFE SERIES

How to Get Out of
THE TRUE SELF TRAP

The Life Changing Secret Of Heroic Stories

Kalinda Rose Stevenson, Ph.D.

ABKA

ABKA Publishing

Copyright © 2014 by Kalinda Rose Stevenson. All rights reserved worldwide.
Published by ABKA Publishing, North Las Vegas, Nevada
ISBN-13: 978-0692249413
ISBN-10: 0692249419

Cover photo from Depositphotos
Cover design by Kalinda Rose Stevenson and James L. Stevenson

No part of this publication may be replicated, redistributed, or given away in any form without the prior written consent of the author/publisher or the terms relayed to you herein.

This publication is designed to provide accurate and authoritative information in regard to the subject matter covered. It is sold with the understanding that the publisher is not engaged in rendering legal, accounting, or other professional services. If legal advice or other expert assistance is required, the services of a competent professional person should be sought.

This volume includes slightly revised versions of a series of blog posts published on KalindaRoseStevenson.com from January 3 to February 18, 2011.

Library of Congress Control Number: 2014944732

What happens in any good story is not that characters change, but rather, their circumstances have forced them to take a new tack, and parts of their character that were previously dormant, suddenly open up and are revealed.

                                                      James Ryan

Free Thank You Bonus

What is your *true self*? What is the relationship of your true self to the world? Every religious and spiritual belief system has answers for these questions. Each offers a vision of your true nature and what you must do to remove obstacles to becoming your true self.

Your **Thank You Bonus** identifies fundamental differences between traditional Christian beliefs and New Age spirituality on these questions.

Is Your True Self Meant to Be An Ant or a Mockingbird? Assumptions in Traditional Christian Religion and New Age Spirituality about Your True Self.

The bonus is available as a downloadable PDF. You can find the download link to the PDF in the References section under Bonus.

Contents

Free Thank You Bonus	vi
Preface	xi
Introduction Two Self Help Models	1

PART 1 TRANSFORMING YOUR LIFE STORIES

Chapter 1 The Power to Change in Your Life Stories	11
Chapter 2 The Power of Stories	13
Chapter 3 Traditional Stories	15
Chapter 4 Life Story Transformation	19
Chapter 5 Obedience to Authority	21

PART 2 YOUR FLAT TIRE STORIES

Chapter 6 Flat Tire Stories	27
Chapter 7 A Life Changing Event or An Occurrence?	31
Chapter 8 Would You Keep the Money?	35
Chapter 9 The Human Story in Your Flat Tire Event	39
Chapter 10 Ready or Not, It's Time to Change Your Life	43

PART 3 WHO ARE YOU IN YOUR STORIES?

Chapter 11 Hero, Bully, Toady, or Victim?	49
Chapter 12 Who Saves Ralphie from the Bully?	51
Chapter 13 The Dream Smashers	55
Chapter 14 When Those You Trust Let You Down	59
Chapter 15 Big Dreams for Grownups	65

PART 4 HOW HEROIC STORIES CHANGE YOUR LIFE

    Chapter 16 Why Do You Need Heroic Stories?   73

    Chapter 17 Who Are You in Your Life Story?   77

    Chapter 18 Amazement and Your Life Stories   81

    Chapter 19 Self-Actualized Individual or Hero?   85

    Chapter 20 You Are Not Alone   87

PART 5 WHAT DO YOUR LIFE STORIES COST?

    Chapter 21 Do You Sell Your Soul for Money?   93

    Chapter 22 Trading the Priceless for Orange Soda   97

    Chapter 23 Soul Sick   101

    Chapter 24 Live It Well   105

    Chapter 25 What Do You Have to Change?   111

PART 6 STORIES ON YOUR LIFE STORYWHEEL

    Chapter 26 Going in Circles on Your Life Storywheel   119

    Chapter 27 Change Your Life by Going in a Straight Line   123

    Chapter 28 Events Transpire to Get You Home   127

    Chapter 29 Alone on Your Own Dark Side of the Moon   131

    Chapter 30 Success after Your Big Dream Dies   135

PART 7 CREATING YOUR LIFE STORIES

    Chapter 31 Be a Storyteller to Transform Your Life Story   143

    Chapter 32 Be the Creator of Your Life Story   149

    Chapter 33 How Long Does It Take?   153

    Chapter 34 From Manipulation to Love   157

    Chapter 35 Life Changing Unconditional Love   161

Conclusion How to Get Out of the True Self Trap	165
About the Author	179
Write a Review	181
References	183
Index	187

Preface

How to Get Out of the True Self Trap originated as a series of blog posts rather than a book. Each series consisted of five blog posts, published Monday through Friday over a seven week period from January 3 to February 18, 2011. The unifying focus of the blog posts was the power of stories to change your life. The blog series ended when I moved from one location to another, and experienced once again the disrupting experiences of packing, moving, unpacking, and getting settled that are necessary tasks involved in moving from one place to another. The blog posts are now gone from my website. However, the unifying themes of stories, creating, focus, and self perception continue to intrigue me.

I have kept the original structure of the posts by treating each post as a separate chapter and each week's posts as a separate part. The original posts have been lightly edited and the order of the parts slightly rearranged.

The *Introduction* and *Conclusion* are new material based on what I have continued to learn about stories, the difference between problem solving and creating, and the importance of focus in creating the life you choose. They also reflect how my own understanding has changed over the course of more than three years. Most significantly, they raise questions about the idea that any of us has a "True Self" hidden away within us.

How to Get Out of the True Self Trap is the first book in an intended series titled **"Heroic Stories to Change Your Life Series."** The purpose of the series is to offer a liberating perspective on creating the life you choose by focusing on heroic stories rather than endless self-analysis.

These short essays offer a different model of how to live the life you choose that doesn't involve getting rid of the parts of you that you consider flawed in a quest to discover your ideal True Self. The real point of these little stories is that you are already capable of more than you imagine.

Introduction

Two Self Help Models

Do you want to live a happier, more successful, more fulfilling life? Are you looking for how to have, be, and do what you truly desire? What strategies and methods have you tried to accomplish your goals and achieve your dreams? Did they help get what you wanted?

If your efforts did not accomplish your goals and achieve your dreams, why didn't they work for you? Why don't you have what you truly desire to have? Why aren't you the person you truly desire to be? Why don't you do what you truly desire to do? What's the secret? What are you missing? What's standing in your way?

Chipping Away the False Self

If you are asking these questions, you have probably heard about Michelangelo's sculpture of David as a metaphor of how to live the life you truly desire to live.

As the story goes, Michelangelo was asked how he made his statue of David. Michelangelo said that it was easy. All he had to do was chip away any part of the stone that didn't look like David.

These words of Michelangelo about carving his statue of David have become a familiar cliché for self help work. If you do a quick Google search, you will find numerous references to the idea that you can discover your *True Self* by chipping away at your *False Self*. Your False Self is the reason why you don't live the life you desire to live. Your False Self blocks you from having, being, and doing what your True Self truly desires. Your False Self prevents you from living the life you want to live.

In the past, I have cited these words of Michelangelo in various articles and blog posts. However, as a metaphor of how to change your life so that you live the kind of life you dream of living, I now believe that this metaphor is flawed. It assumes that your True Self exists in some sort of changeless form within you. It is trapped and must be set free by getting rid of your False Self. This metaphor to discover your True Self becomes a ridding process. If you get rid of your False Self, you will liberate your True Self, and then you can have what you want.

Why are True Self and False Self capitalized here? By convention, personal names are capitalized. If you really do have a fully formed True Self trapped inside you, it deserves to have a personal name, just as the self that is blocking your True Self deserves to be called your False Self. The purpose of the capitalization of these terms in the *Introduction* and *Conclusion* is to call attention to the question: Does your True Self exist as an *archetype* in some sort of changeless form?

Is Your True Self Changeless?

An archetype is the original form of something. In his masterful study, *The Passion of the Western Mind: Understanding the Ideas That Have Shaped Our World View*, Richard Tarnas makes this claim:

> Our way of thinking is still profoundly Greek in its underlying logic, so much so that before we can begin to grasp the character of our own thought, we must first look closely at that of the Greeks (Tarnas 2).

Michelangelo's belief that a perfect David was hidden within the stone was deeply grounded in this Greek worldview of archetypal forms. What Michelangelo said about David is what he said about all of his statues:

> Every block of stone has a statue inside it and it is the task of the sculptor to discover it.

The relevant question is: Does this metaphor truly help you become happier, more successful, and more fulfilled or does it distract you from accomplishing your goals? I have come to realize how much this metaphor itself is more of an obstacle rather than a solution to becoming happier, more successful, and more fulfilled.

Looking for the Ideal You

To see why the metaphor itself is part of what holds you back, we need to look a little more closely at the metaphor itself in the context of Greek philosophy. If Tarnas is correct that "our way of thinking is still profoundly Greek," it's worth the effort to begin with what Tarnas considers as the defining basis of Greek philosophy. Tarnas begins with Plato's vision of the world:

> At its basis was a view of the cosmos as an ordered expression of certain primordial essences or transcendent first principles, variously conceived as Forms, Ideas, universals, changeless absolutes, immortal deities, divine archai, and archetypes (Tarnas 3).

The unseen *Form* or *Idea* does not have the same meaning for Plato as it does in contemporary English connotations of the word *idea*. In English, an idea is a thought or concept or a notion. It's something you can imagine in your mind. It isn't something that has its own existence as an entity.

For Plato, the *Idea* is not simply an abstract thought or concept about the nature of something. The Form or Idea is real. It's the template for what you observe in the material world.

In other words, reality exists in two planes: the material world and the non-material world. The material world is what we experience with our senses. In contrast, the non-material world is where the unchanging, permanent Form or Idea of something exists. Everything you experience with your senses in the material world exists in its primary form in the ideal plane.

The Idea or Form in the non-material world is more real than visible objects in the material world because the Idea or Form came first. Without the template, we would not be able to recognize what we observe in the material world.

This is why you can recognize a cat as a cat. Although no two cats are identical — even cats of the same breed —

the Idea of Cat on the Ideal plane allows you to recognize any cat as a cat.

Tarnas claims that Plato's perspective on archetypal Forms or Ideas is the foundation for the evolution of the Western mind (Tarnas 4).

Can You Discover Your True Self?

Why is this heavy-duty philosophy relevant for you and your quest to become your true self? It's all heady stuff and raises many questions.

How well does this Platonic notion of changeless, permanent Forms or Ideas in the non-material Ideal plane help you live your life the material world?

How does the idea of Michelangelo chipping away at what was "Not David" to discover David hidden within help you live a creative, happy, successful life or does the quest itself prevent you from being successful, happy, and fulfilled?

Do you need a better perspective than this metaphor about an ideal David trapped in stone?

A Heroic Story Perspective

The purpose of *How to Get out of the True Self Trap: The Life Changing Secret of Heroic Stories* is to offer a different perspective. Rather than work to chip away your False Self to free your perfect True Self trapped within you, heroic stories can offer you perspectives on who you are and who you can become that are truly life changing.

The epigraph by James Ryan captures the essence of the difference between a quest to find your True Self by chipping away at what you consider your False Self and the experience of discovering hidden facets of yourself that you never knew you had:

> What happens in any good story is not that characters change, but rather, their circumstances have forced them to take a new tack, and parts of their character that were previously dormant, suddenly open up and are revealed.

Much self help work is based on the assumption that something is wrong with you. Therefore, the solution is to get rid of parts of you that are flawed, to set free the Real You hidden away somewhere inside you. It becomes a process of chipping away your False Self to find your True Self.

In contrast, heroic stories don't treat you as a problem to be solved. Rather, the best stories teach you to be creative, resourceful, powerful, and capable of accomplishing truly great things. Stories teach you to discover hidden potentials within yourself.

The short essays that follow originated as a series of blog posts rather than a book. They offer a different model of how to live the life you choose that doesn't involve chipping away at the parts of you that are somehow flawed. The real point of these little stories is that you are already capable of more than you imagine you can be.

Part 1

Transforming

Your Life Stories

Originally Published January 3-7, 2011

KalindaRoseStevenson.com

Chapter 1

The Power to Change in Your Life Stories

It's that time of year again. It's the New Year, a time when most of us resolve that this year will be different. This is the year that we will finally make more money, get out of debt, lose weight, exercise more, eat better, read books, write books, mend broken relationships...the list goes on and on.

And each year, the hope-filled resolutions don't last very long. Why? Is it lack of discipline? Lack of resolve? Were the plans too big? Something wrong with our mindsets? Our emotions? Our skills?

Maybe the real problem lies elsewhere.

The One Who Tells the Stories

One of the most powerful statements I have ever read is this Hopi Proverb:

> The one who tells the stories rules the world.

This statement is profound in its grasp of the importance of stories as instruments of power. But the real power of stories goes one step further. The one who tells the stories rules the world, and the stories you tell yourself are the most powerful rulers of all.

Storyteller of Your Life Story

The power to change your life story begins with the stories you tell yourself that rule your life. Wherever those stories came from and whoever told them to you first, they rule your life because you have made these stories your own. You have become your own storyteller and the stories you tell yourself rule your life.

What kind of stories are you telling yourself? This is the real question. Are they stories that empower you to fulfill your dreams and accomplish your goals or are they stories that that keep you stuck and struggling?

Chapter 2

The Power of Stories

Why do stories have the power to rule your life? The most important function of stories is to answer the question "why?" Stories answer life's biggest questions. Stories tell you what's important, they teach you who you are, and they teach you how you are to live. This is why identifying the stories you live by is the key to the power to change your life.

What Are Your Life Stories?

At the beginning of this New Year, as you think about your life and the changes you want to make, it's not enough to simply focus on actions, beliefs, and feelings. It's time to dig deeper and identity the stories that lurk beneath the surface of your actions, beliefs, and feelings and ask questions about what you find.

What are your life stories? Where did they come from? Then ask the most important questions of all. Do your stories serve you? Or do you serve your stories? Do your stories help you achieve success in life? Or do your stories block your success in life?

Your Stories and Your Success in Life

Whatever you are trying to change in your life, you will find that there is a story attached to it. If you can transform the stories that do not serve you, you can change your life to achieve the success in life you are seeking.

Chapter 3

Traditional Stories

Do the traditional stories that rule your life allow you to be true to yourself? For many of us, the stories we tell ourselves are not authentic stories, because they do not emerge from knowledge of our authentic selves—our authentic selves with their dormant capacities that are capable of doing far more than we have ever imagined.

Instead, they are traditional stories, based on family stories, passed through the generations. They are stories based on conventional wisdom within our cultural, national, and ethnic groups. They are stories based on religious beliefs.

We inherit these traditional stories as they are passed down through families, cultures, nations, and religions. One of the strongest themes of these inherited stories is obedience to authority.

When Stories Don't Fit

The effect is that these inherited stories are like well-worn hand-me-down shoes that are too small and hurt our feet.

But we wear them anyway and hobble through life, wearing someone else's old shoes, living out of inherited traditional stories that do not allow us to live authentic lives.

What is the effect of living your life ruled by stories that don't fit you? You can set as many goals as you want, make as many plans as you want, try as hard as you can, but if you don't pay attention to the stories that rule your life, you are fighting a losing battle. The stories will rule you until you decide to rule your stories. You cannot be true to yourself if you must obey old stories that hobble you with old belief systems.

Stuck in a Rut

What is the result of these efforts to wear inherited stories that don't fit your authentic self? One of my friends has told me several times that her gravestone will read:

> She never got it put together.

With these words, my friend expresses in words the high cost of using inherited stories to define the *Why?* of her life. She also—unwittingly—demonstrates how her own self-told stories diminish her, demean her, and rob her of the power to live the authentic life she truly desires to live. What is the "it" she never got put together?

Chapter 4

Life Story Transformation

How can you change your life when you go through life with the same nagging thoughts? Will I ever get it put together? What must I do to change my life? Will I truly live before I die?

When you feel stuck and struggling, when nothing you do ever seems to make a difference, it's time to set yourself free from old belief systems based on traditional stories and inherited family stories.

The most powerful transformation process to change your life is to replace the stories you inherited with authentic life stories.

What Are Authentic Life Stories?

What are authentic stories? Authentic stories are original stories, rather than traditional stories you learned without ever choosing to make them your own.

The word *authentic* is derived from the Greek word, *authentikos,* which has the sense of acting on your own authority (*Online Etymology,* "authentic").

The connection between living an authentic life and the ability to act on your own authority is the core of the process of changing your life by changing your stories.

This means that the question of authority is a critical factor in discovering how to live your own authentic life.

Know Yourself

The critical point is that there is a direct connection between knowing who you are and the stories you tell yourself about your life.

The wisest words ever spoken in human history are these from the Temple of Apollo at Delphi: *know yourself.* You cannot live authentically if you don't know who you are.

You can change your life by transforming the inherited stories that keep you stuck and struggling into stories that allow you to create and live your own authentic life story.

Chapter 5

Obedience to Authority

Transforming your life stories begins with this claim:

> If you claim the authority to live your life according to your own authentic stories, based on knowing who you really are, the result can transform your life.

Notice carefully that the process begins with the relationship between *authority* and *authentic*.

It's a bit tricky to compare the two words directly, since *authority* is derived from Latin and *authentic* is derived from Greek, and both words have developed ranges of meaning in English over the centuries. Comparison is also a bit tricky because *authority* is a noun and *authentic* is an adjective.

But if we look at these two definitions from the *Online Etymology Dictionary*, we can see that the real difference between these two words concerns the location of authority.

Auctoritas is "invention, advice, opinion, influence, command," from *auctor* "master, leader, author"...meaning "power to enforce obedience (*Online Etymology*, "authority").

Authentic is derived from the Greek *authentikos* "original, genuine, principal," from *authentes*, "one acting on one's own authority," from *autos* "self" + *hentes* "doer, being..." (*Online Etymology*, "authentic").

If you have authority, you have the power to force others to obey you. If you are authentic, you have the power to act on your own authority.

The Location of Authority

Based on this distinction, the critical difference between the *inauthentic stories* that rule your life and the *authentic stories* concerns the location of authority.

This means the core issue in the process of transforming your life stories is the question of obedience. Are you free to be your own authority or must you obey external authority?

The crux of the problem is expressed in one of my all-time favorite quotations. It's spoken in the episode, "The Novocaine Mutiny" in the M*A*S*H TV show by the power-hungry surgeon, Major Frank Burns:

As I see it, unless we each conform, unless we obey orders, unless we follow our leaders blindly, there is no possible way we can remain free" (Burns).

The statement is absurd on the surface of it. What makes the statement especially relevant to the process of changing your life stories is the utter lack of self-awareness of the speaker.

Obedience or Authentic Life Choices?

It's one thing for a character in a TV series to utter contradictory nonsense. It's another matter for the rest of us to go through life blindly surrendering our authentic lives to the authority of others. Yet this is exactly why "the one who tells the stories rules the world" is such a powerful insight into the difference between blind obedience and authentic life choices.

The only way to live authentically is to claim the authority to live by stories that allow you to know yourself and make your own life choices.

However, when you claim the authority to choose your own life stories, the process of living an authentic life can get tough. This is particularly true for people who come from backgrounds that emphasize obedience to authority as the only true life path.

Part 2

Your Flat Tire Stories

Originally Published January 10-14, 2011

KalindaRoseStevenson.com

Chapter 6

Flat Tire Stories

Stories have power to change your life for the simple reason that stories are about life changes.

What makes a story a story? The one-word answer is *change*. Something changes and someone has to respond to the change. Stories are about some sort of event that jolts you out of ordinary experience and forces you to do something different.

If you get up in the morning, eat breakfast, go to work, and do exactly what you did the day before, you don't have to think differently or do anything you haven't done before. You end the day the way you began. You are unchanged. You have no story to tell.

But if you get up in the morning, eat breakfast, and go to work, and on the way to work, your car gets a flat tire, something has changed in your normal routine.

Now you have a story to tell. "Because this happened, something else happened and then something else happened."

The flat tire initiated a stream of events, all connected to the original event: your car got a flat tire.

Did the Flat Tire Change You?

From the perspective of a story, the most important part of the story is not the event that caused this cascading stream of other events. The most important part of the story is what you did in response to the event.

Did you change the tire? Did you call for help? Did you wait helplessly by the side of the road? Did you get grease on your new clothes? Did you have a temper tantrum?

Whatever happened, the life changing story is not what happened but how you responded to what happened. You had to react in some way to this event and your reaction changed you in some way.

The Essence of Story

The experience of change in response to unexpected events is also the essence of life itself. Life is full of unexpected events that force us to respond in some way.

Unexpected events are also the essence of a story. Something happens and someone changes because of what happened. This definition of story also means that stories are not simply observations or recitations of occurrences.

I remember a friend who would say things like: "I saw Mrs. Hanson walking down the street today." I would wait for a story to follow this statement only to realize after a moment or two that there was nothing else. My friend was simply making a statement that she saw someone walking down the street. Nothing happened to change either Mrs. Hanson or my friend. There was no story.

Your Life Story Is Created by Flat Tires

The truth is, life is a series of flat tire events — occurrences you didn't expect that require you to respond in some way. Some flat tire events are minor annoyances. Some are catastrophes. Some are actually wonderful opportunities. Some are painful experiences.

The story of your life — the story you tell yourself and others about your life — is made up of your responses to your unexpected flat tire events.

Chapter 7

A Life Changing Event or An Occurrence?

A *flat tire* is a metaphor for some unexpected occurrence that intrudes into your ordinary life and forces you to respond somehow.

Our lives are filled with flat tires. But is every flat tire an event that triggers some sort of change in your life? It depends on whether your flat tire is an occurrence or an event.

A flat tire occurrence is something that requires you to react in some way but does not require you to change. In contrast, a flat tire event forces you to change your life in some way.

No Big Deal

Let's go back to the original scenario. You get up. You eat breakfast. On your way to work, your car has a flat tire. The flat tire doesn't have to be a big deal. You have a spare. You have the tools. You have a jack. You've changed tires before. So, you get out of your car. You change the tire. It takes only a few minutes. After you change the tire, you drive to work and still get there on time.

This is an occurrence. You might mention it to other people but it is very unlikely you will spend the rest of the day at the water cooler talking about it.

No Story Here

There's no story in this flat tire because you didn't have to make any life changing decisions. You didn't have to learn anything new. You didn't have to do anything scary or difficult. You did what most of us do in our lives.

Most of the time, we deal with tasks, problems, and situations as they come up. We go on with our lives, doing what we need to do when we need to do it.

This is ordinary life. No one is going to make a movie about someone who has a flat tire, changes the tire with no complications, and then goes on to work. There's no life changing story event in this. This is just a flat tire.

A Flat Tire Event

What turns a flat tire into a flat tire event? Anything that takes you out of your ordinary competence and forces you to do something you have never done before is a *flat tire event*. When the metaphorical flat tire puts you in danger and you feel frightened, you are experiencing a flat tire event. When the flat tire forces you to confront your greatest fears, this is a flat tire event. This is when your life is about to change one way or another. This is when the story starts.

Chapter 8

Would You Keep the Money?

Let's consider the life changing potential of a flat tire event with another imagined scenario about you and your flat tire.

Once again, you are on your way to work when your car has a flat tire. You pull off the road and make a call to your road service company.

While you are waiting, you get out of the car and walk around a bit, to calm your nerves as you wait impatiently for the tow truck to arrive. Then you notice something behind a bush beside the road. You go over to investigate. What do you find?

What kind of story do you want? Do you want some tough choices? Let's start with something simple.

No Challenge

You see a small rock. It's granite. The mica flecks glint in the sunlight. You like to collect rocks, so you pick it up and put it in your pocket. You say to yourself, this can go on the shelf near the front window. Just then, the tow truck arrives. You go back to your car. The spare is put on your car. Off you go to work.

I agree. It's not much of a story because there was no challenge. This is not a life changing story.

Let's try again with something more interesting.

The Three Dollar Challenge

You see something behind the bush. You go to investigate. What do you see? You see a wallet. You pick up the wallet and look inside. Imagine your surprise to discover the driver's license of your best friend. You count the cash. Three one dollar bills.

Now ask yourself: Would you return this wallet with three dollars to your best friend? Or would you keep the money and throw away the wallet along with the driver's license? Would you tell your best friend you found it?

Once again, this isn't much of a life changing story. These are not difficult ethical decisions. Three dollars isn't much money. You return the wallet and cash to your friend. Maybe your friend can explain how the wallet got behind that bush by the side of the road. You can both marvel over the odds that you would be the one to find it.

Let's make this story more interesting.

The Three Thousand Dollar Challenge

You find a different wallet. This one is bulging with cash. You count the cash. Thirty crisp, new one-hundred dollars bills. Three thousand dollars. You look at the driver's license and study the photo.

How much challenge do you want?

Let's imagine that the face in the photo is someone who is dramatically "other" than you are. Whatever your race, your age, your ethnic identity, your sex, your height, your weight, your hair color, your eye color, the person in the photo is as unlike you as it's possible to be. You recognize your own bias and prejudice against this "other" person. How about if you imagine the last person on this Earth you would willingly help? That is the person whose face is on the driver's license in front of you.

Now what do you do? You have three thousand dollars in cash in a wallet belonging to someone you hate. Do you go to the police? Do you attempt to contact the owner? Do you keep the cash?

An Answer to Prayer?

Let's add another factor. What if you are broke and you really need the money? You got a flat tire because your tires are bald. You can't pay your bills. You can't buy food. What if you need exactly three thousand dollars and you have to have it today?

What if you have been praying and praying and praying for help. Has God answered your prayers by leading you to this wallet by the side of the road? Does God intend for you to keep the money even though it really belongs to someone else? Even if you know the identity of the owner of the wallet?

When Flat Tire Events Force Ethical Decisions

These are enough *what if* questions to get to the real point: flat tire events become life changing stories when they force you to make ethical decisions.

Chapter 9

The Human Story in Your Flat Tire Event

The most powerful metaphorical flat tire event connects you with the essence of the human story.

Human stories evoke universal experiences that transcend any limitations of race, sex, age, geography, social status, and everything else that causes human beings to see ourselves as somehow different and separate and better than other people.

Human stories force us to dig beneath what separates us into tribes, families, castes, sects, and nations to experience what binds us all into one common humanity.

Human stories plunge us into universal human emotions such as love and hate, trust and fear, joy and sorrow, generosity and greed.

At the same time, any human story that begins with a flat tire event is unique, particular, and immersed in its own time and place and culture.

The Hero's Journey Archetype

When your flat tire event does this, it becomes an archetypal story. The word *archetype* means *original pattern*, derived from the Greek *archon* (first) and *typos* (pattern) *(Online Etymology, "archetype")*.

The two people who did the most to connect the idea of archetypes and stories were Carl Jung and Joseph Campbell. Both Jung and Campbell identified a type of archetypal story called *the hero's journey* (Jung, archetypes; Campbell, *hero*).

The hero's journey story, with its dual emphasis on what it means to be a hero and why heroic stories are journey stories, is central to transforming your life stories.

The Wallet by the Side of the Road

Before we get to the hero's journey, let's go back to the wallet you found by the side of the road.

Finding a wallet with three dollars and your best friend's ID is not very likely to precipitate a life changing journey because it probably won't stir up many conflicting emotions, such as greed and desire in conflict with your responsibility to your friend.

However, finding a wallet with three thousand dollars and the ID of someone who is totally "other" is rife with potential to change your life forever because it brings to the surface universal human emotions.

Unless you are wealthy enough that three thousand dollars is chump change, this is enough cash to stir up all kinds of emotions about money, ranging from greed and envy to a desire to do the right thing, even if you're broke and desperately need money.

If these conflicting emotions about money aren't enough for you, you also know that the money belongs to someone who is "other" than you.

When you add strong emotions of distrust, hate, prejudice, and xenophobia to your emotional stew about money, the combination is enough to create ethical, emotional, and spiritual conflict in just about all of us.

So you stand by the side of the road, holding the wallet with three thousand dollars and the ID of the "other" in your hand, knowing that no one except you knows you have it. What do you do? Whatever you decide, the decision will change you one way or another.

Chapter 10

Ready or Not, It's Time to Change Your Life

The most significant feature of a flat tire event that can change your life is that you're never ready for it. That's the thing about flat tires. You're driving along, minding your own business, when suddenly, unexpectedly, your tire goes flat. Maybe it's a sudden blowout, which can be a frightening experience when you're behind the wheel. Or maybe it's less dramatic but no less urgent. While you were on your way to some destination, something happened to one of the tires that was taking you there.

The unexpected nature of the flat tire demonstrates the point of John Lennon's words from his song, "Beautiful Boy":

> Life is what happens to you while you're busy making other plans (Lennon).

Do It Now

The second defining feature of a flat tire event is its urgency. You can only drive so far on a flat tire and then you have to do something about it. You can't procrastinate, put it off, or wait until "someday" to deal with it.

These two defining characteristics of a flat tire are the essential features of any metaphorical flat tire event. You didn't expect it and you have to do something about it right now.

These two facts lead to the third reality of a flat tire event.

You're Never Ready

You aren't ready. Even if you do your best to live by the Boy Scout motto, *Be Prepared,* you're never ready for the kind of experience that qualifies as a true flat tire event.

Consider the words of the founder of the Boy Scouts, Lord Baden-Powell:

> "Be prepared for what?" someone once asked Baden-Powell, the founder of Scouting.
>
> "Why, for any old thing," said Baden-Powell (Baden-Powell).

That's the challenge at the beginning of a true hero's journey. You might be prepared for "any old thing" but you're not prepared for this new thing. This is beginning point of a hero's journey. You're not a hero at the beginning of your journey because you are not ready to be a hero.

If you have a flat tire, and you have a jack and a spare in the trunk, and you deal with it as just one of life's annoyances, there's nothing in the experience that's going to set you off on your life changing story experience.

Your Decision

A true flat tire event is an urgent occurrence you didn't expect and you are definitely not ready for it. But here it is. The moment of decision. Do you start the hero's journey or not?

In his insightful book, *Stealing Fire from the Gods*, James Bonnet makes this statement about preparedness:

> In great stories, ninety-nine out of a hundred heroes take up the challenge. In real life, the vast majority refuse. To refuse the call means to let the problems slide and not become part of the solution. The world remains in trouble and we remain stuck (Bonnet 128).

You can't drive very far on a flat tire and you can't get unstuck if you don't fix the metaphorical flat tires of your life. You can sit by the side of the road, lamenting your fate, waiting for someone to come along and rescue you, or you can fix the thing yourself.

It's the same with life. You do what you need to do to fix it or you wait helplessly for someone to save you.

This is why changing your life means making a choice to do what you are not ready to do. It means starting out on your own heroic journey to transform your life.

Enough Preparation

And this is enough preparation for the process to transform your life by transforming your life stories. The remaining five Parts use favorite movies as examples of the hero's journey required to change your life by transforming your life stories.

Part 3

Who Are You in Your Stories?

Originally Published January 17-21, 2011

KalindaRoseStevenson.com

Chapter 11

Hero, Bully, Toady, or Victim?

If you want to change your life, the place to begin is by figuring out who you are in your life story.

In one of my favorite movies, *A Christmas Story*, young Ralphie wants an official "Red Ryder 200-shot Carbine Action Air Rifle" for Christmas (*Christmas Story*).

We find out why Ralphie wants the air rifle in one of his fantasy sequences. Ralphie, dressed in full Hollywood cowboy regalia, saves his family from attack by the dreaded Black Bart and his gang. While Dad, Mom, and younger brother, Randy, cower helplessly under the kitchen table, Ralphie uses his trusty air rifle to save them.

Hero or Victim?

In his fantasy, Ralphie imagines himself as the hero. This is why he wants the air rifle. Ralphie wants to be a hero. Fantasy Ralphie is fearless, able to ward off danger, save his family, and be recognized for his heroics by his grateful family.

We soon find out that Ralphie is something else in the real world. The voiceover of the adult Ralph explains the three roles for children in Ralphie's world: a bully; a toady; or a victim. There are no child heroes in Ralphie's real world.

We discover that Ralphie and his friends are victims of an older boy who torments the younger boys every day as they walk to and from school. The bully, Scut Farkus, is abetted by a much younger toady, Grover Dill.

The fantasy cowboy hero with his air rifle is actually the frightened victim of a neighborhood bully. The ones who cower in fear are the victims of the bully.

Chapter 12

Who Saves Ralphie from the Bully?

The question, Who saves Ralphie from the bully?, introduces the most important word in any heroic story—*saves*. Someone needs to be saved from someone or something. This means that heroic stories are salvation stories and every hero is a savior.

Who is Ralphie in *A Christmas Story*? The narrator tells us that children in Ralphie's world have three roles to play. They are bullies, toadies, or victims. The missing role in this list is the hero, the one who saves the victims from the bullies and puts the toadies in their place.

Who Saves Ralphie?

Who saves Ralphie from the bully, Scut Farkus? Although *A Christmas Story* is not usually on lists of hero's journey stories, Ralphie becomes his own hero when he believes that his dream of getting his official Red Ryder 200-shot Carbine Action Air Rifle for Christmas is shattered.

In that despondent moment, Scut pelts Ralphie with a snowball. In the moments that follow, as Scut taunts and laughs at his victim, something happens within Ralphie:

> Deep in the recesses of my brain, a tiny red hot little flame began to grow.

Ralphie is no longer willing to be the bully's victim. Ralphie beats up Scut Farkus in a fit of rage, while spewing an endless stream of profanity:

> Something had happened. A fuse blew. I had gone out of my skull.

> I have since heard of people in extreme duress speaking in strange tongues. I became conscious that a steady torrent of swearing and obscenities of all kinds was pouring out of me as I screamed.

Impelled by his own outrage, Ralphie becomes his own hero to save himself from the bully.

Hero's Journeys as David and Goliath Stories

The defining characteristic of any hero's journey story is that heroes have to save themselves by confronting their greatest adversary.

From a story perspective, any hero's journey story is some form of a David and Goliath story. The adversary is always someone or something bigger, stronger, and more powerful than the hero.

In Ralphie's hero's journey, the smaller boy Ralphie, who is used to being Scut's victim, beats up the bigger boy in full view of the toady, Grover Dill, and the other victim children. The bully is not only defeated but publicly humiliated in front of his victims.

The victim has become his own savior.

The Rescue of the Hero

It's also true in heroic stories that the hero who has confronted the bully and prevailed is often so wounded, exhausted, or overcome that the hero needs to be rescued. In *The Hero with a Thousand Faces,* Joseph Campbell calls this the "rescue from without" when "the world may have to come and get him" (Campbell 207).

In Ralphie's case, his mother comes to get him, takes him home, and calms him down after his confrontation with the bully. But his mother didn't save him from the bully. Ralphie had to be a hero to save himself. Ralphie stopped playing the victim role and became his own savior.

Waiting for Salvation

One of the reasons that *A Christmas Story* is so powerful is that it reveals so much about the enduring truth of childhood for most of us. Most of us learned to be the victims, waiting to be saved from bullies. We had very little training in how to be our own heroes and save ourselves.

To truly change your life, you must become the hero in your own life story and save yourself from your greatest adversary.

Chapter 13

The Dream Smashers

In *A Christmas Story,* Ralphie has a big dream. He wants to get his official Red Ryder 200-shot Carbine Action Air Rifle for Christmas so he can be the hero he imagines himself to be.

He has his own vision of himself as the hero. His fantasy is not about getting an air rifle to bully people. He is not Scut Farkus. There is no desire to use the BB gun to hurt people—except the bad guys of course—or to bully others. In Ralphie's heroic vision of himself, he will save his family from marauders. He will be brave. He will be the center of attention.

Ralphie's Big Dream and the Dream Smashers

But Ralphie has a hard time keeping his big dream alive because of the dream smashers around him. Who are the dream smashers? They are the adults who keep responding to his desire to get a Red Ryder air rifle for Christmas with the dire warning: "You'll shoot your eye out."

His mother. His teacher, Miss Shields. Even Santa Claus himself. They all tell him that the thing he wants more than anything in his life is too dangerous for him.

But Ralphie is driven by his dream to have his Red Ryder air rifle, which means he has to convince the dream-smashing adults in his world to give him one.

Ralphie devises actions to fulfill his dreams. He puts an ad for a Red Ryder gun in his mother's magazine. The plan fails. His mother doesn't want him to have one. She says: "You'll shoot your eye out."

He writes what he is sure is a brilliant theme to persuade his teacher of the merits of a Red Ryder air rifle. That plan fails when she grades his brilliant theme with a C+ and the dreaded warning at the bottom of the page: "P.S. You'll shoot your eye out."

Finally, Ralphie takes his appeal to the top. He asks Santa Claus at the local department store. He has both a humiliating and terrifying experience. But Ralphie manages to make one final appeal to the big guy. What is his reward? Santa's boot in his face and the dreaded warning: "You'll shoot your eye out, kid."

In a world in which children are bullies, toadies, or victims, Ralphie finds his dream to be a hero smashed again and again with the warning that tells Ralphie: Your heroic dream is too dangerous. Don't want what you want. You'll get hurt.

What Happened to Your Big Dreams?

In *Stealing Fire from the Gods,* James Bonnet makes this claim:

> In great stories, ninety-nine out of a hundred heroes take up the challenge. In real life, the vast majority refuse. To refuse the call means to let the problems slide and not become part of the solution. The world remains in trouble and we remain stuck" (Bonnet 128).

Do you suppose that there's a direct connection between "you'll shoot your eye out, kid" and the refusal to take up the heroic challenge?

What happens to children with big dreams who continually have their dreams squelched, squashed, and shattered with a warning not to take the risk—because you'll get hurt if you attempt to be a hero?

What happened to you and your dreams? Were they squelched by the dream smashers who responded to your dreams with warnings? Don't do it! Be careful! You might get hurt!

Chapter 14

When Those You Trust Let You Down

What do you do when those you trust let you down? *A Christmas Story* also demonstrates how the adult world betrays young Ralphie's trust. There are two specific moments of betrayal in the movie. Both involve shattering of a belief perpetrated by the adult world on trusting children who don't know any better.

Little Orphan Annie's Secret Society

The first is Ralphie's experience with the Little Orphan Annie decoder pin. Back in the pre-television days, children listened to serials on the radio. Ralphie's favorite show was "Little Orphan Annie"—a show sponsored by Ovaltine.

Ralphie's desire to have the decoder pin is all part of his heroic dreams. When he becomes part of Little Orphan Annie's secret society, he can be part of her efforts to save people in need.

Annie Is Depending on You

Ralphie "drank gallons of Ovaltine" so he could send off the Ovaltine inner seal to get his decoder pin. He can barely contain his excitement when he gets his decoder pin, becomes part of Annie's secret society, and receives his first secret message.

The message is delivered with a stern warning by the announcer: "Remember, Annie is depending on you." The announcer also insists that the members must keep the secret.

These two commands remind Ralphie that he must be worthy of the trust that comes with membership in Little Orphan Annie's Secret Society. They are commands to a trusting child who believes that he is about to discover a big secret and that the secret matters. Ralphie wonders if the "the fate of the planet hangs in the balance."

The Secret Message Decoded

Ralphie does his best to be trustworthy and keep the secret. He rushes to the bathroom where he can decode the secret message in private.

But what does Ralphie discover about this urgent appeal from Annie for his help? The urgent message that must be kept secret? The urgent message that only members must know? Ralphie is stunned to realize that the secret message is nothing more than "a crummy commercial":

Be sure to drink your Ovaltine.

Ralphie's tenure as a trusted and trusting member of Little Orphan Annie's Secret Society ends when he leaves his decoder pin and decoded message in plain view on the bathroom hamper. He leaves the bathroom, a betrayed child:

I went out to face the world again. Wiser.

Betrayed by Santa Claus

The other notable example of betrayed trust is Ralphie's encounter with the department store Santa Claus. Ralphie is already old enough and aware enough to be skeptical about Santa Claus, but Ralphie is willing to suspend his own disbelief in his quest for his Red Ryder air rifle.

Ralphie's experience with the child-hating, sadistic Santa Claus of *A Christmas Story* is another betrayal of trust. Not only Ralphie, but every other child who waits in a long line to see Santa is reduced to a terrified, disillusioned child.

A Painful Path to Wisdom

The harsh reality of life is that the passage from childhood to adulthood is filled with such moments when children discover that the adult world has been lying to them with stories about Santa Claus, the Easter Bunny, and the Tooth Fairy, among others. It's a painful path to wisdom.

When I discovered the truth about Santa Claus, I felt such a sense of betrayal at the collusion of the adults in my little world—my parents, my teachers, my Sunday school teachers, the local state representative who called children in the town claiming to be Santa Claus—that I decided that I would never do that to my own children. Although I know that I am in the minority, I have long thought that children deserve better than this. But my objections to Santa Claus take me off my point here.

My point is that every life is filled with moments of awareness when you realize that your trust has been betrayed by stories told you to by those you trusted.

The Challenge

When you realize that you have been deceived by someone you thought you could trust, the real challenge is to trust yourself even when others let you down. To respond to cynicism with a heroic vision. To meet every betrayal with a renewed intention to tell the truth. This is all part of the heroic journey to change your life by transforming your life stories.

Chapter 15

Big Dreams for Grownups

Of all the stories about the hero's journey, why begin with *A Christmas Story*? Why not begin with an analysis of Joseph Campbell's hero's journey? Why not start with obvious hero's journey stories, such as *Star Wars* or *Indiana Jones*?

Ralphie, the Ordinary Child

It's because Ralphie is an ordinary child. There's nothing much remarkable about Ralphie. He's an ordinary boy who wants to get an air rifle for Christmas. Ralphie is no Harry Potter, boy wizard. He has no magical powers to transform his life. He doesn't have a magic wand and a magic cloak, in a school where he learns the magic arts of transformation. He has no reputation that sets him apart, even from birth. Not Ralphie.

An Ordinary Childhood

For those who romanticize childhood as a time of bliss and innocence, *A Christmas Story* reveals that childhood is often filled with terrors and disappointments and betrayals.

Ralphie's experiences demonstrate the incomprehensible inconsistencies of the adult world and the foibles and mistakes of parents who often get it wrong with their children, even if they mean well, and especially when they behave badly. Ralphie's father, who "weaves a tapestry" of profanity in his battles with the furnace, scares his children with his rantings.

Ralphie gets in trouble for things he didn't do. He gets punished for speaking aloud a word that he hears his father speak every day.

And yet, it's the "Old Man" who buys the Red Ryder 200-shot Carbine Action Air Rifle for Ralphie, the "greatest Christmas gift I have ever received or would ever receive."

The Dreams of Mom and the "Old Man"

The adult characters in *A Christmas Story* are also people who are living ordinary lives, stuck in life stories that don't allow them much room to be heroic. This is especially true for Ralphie's mother. We know that the Old Man has his dreams of winning the contests he enters. We also know that he goes to battle every day with the furnace. We have no idea if Mom has any dreams at all. She loves her children and hates the lamp that the Old Man won as a "major award." But beyond that, we really don't know anything about her dreams.

A Boy Story

It's also worth pointing out that this is a story about a little boy, not a little girl. Even now, most heroic stories are about boys and grown men. Joseph Campbell's model for the hero's journey is a model for men, not women. Men are the saviors. Women are the ones who have to be saved or attained, or the ones who tempt the hero to abandon his journey.

Why Begin the Hero's Journey with Ralphie?

And so I return to the question: Why begin considering the model of the hero's journey with this story of Ralphie and his big dream to get a Red Ryder air rifle for Christmas?

It's the ordinariness of Ralphie that makes this story the place to begin. This is what most of us face when we find ourselves stuck, wanting to change our lives but not quite knowing how to do it.

For those of us who are past childhood, Ralphie's story captures the essence of the problem. Even a childhood dream for something as ordinary as a BB gun is often beyond the reach of children.

For those of us who were never little boys, it also reveals the challenge of how to find our authentic selves in the heroic stories of little boys and grown men.

Big Dreams, Small Abilities

This story of Ralphie who wanted an air rifle for Christmas is the universal story of children everywhere. We have big dreams long before we are capable of accomplishing them.

To change your life, the place to begin is with the stories you heard as a child. What did those stories teach you? What power do they still hold over you? What are your big dreams that you are now capable of accomplishing that you couldn't accomplish as a child?

You Can Accomplish Your Big Dreams

This is the biggest difference between Ralphie and you. Ralphie was a child, without the money or permission to buy the Red Ryder air rifle for himself. He could only get his air rifle as a gift.

This is the real point of all of this. You are no longer a child. You are no longer dependent on someone else to give you what you want. You no longer need permission. You no longer need to wheedle, cajole, ask for, or beg for what you want. You have powers and resources that a child doesn't have. You have the freedom to accomplish your big dreams as a grownup.

Part 4

How Heroic Stories Change Your Life

Originally Published January 24-28, 2011

KalindaRoseStevenson.com

Chapter 16

Why Do You Need Heroic Stories?

Recently, someone asked me what I'm doing these days. I said that I'm writing about changing lives with stories. She said, "Oh, you mean reframing." Actually, I don't mean "reframing." I really mean *stories*.

What Is A Story?

Story is an English word that has multiple meanings. Your definition of story is particularly significant in an era that is as cynical as ours, when the word "story" often refers to something you made up as an excuse for why you didn't do something you promised to do. The basic definition of story is "an account of some happening." The word story is derived from Latin *historia*. (*Online Etymology*, "story").

What's the Problem?

A story is about some event. Something happens that leads to some sort of response. A *heroic story* is a narrative about solving an urgent problem created by a threat. The problem is a flat tire event that cannot be ignored. A heroic story describes the events and actions of the hero to solve the problem and end the threat.

In heroic stories, solving the problem is not easy. Facing the challenges, solving the problem and ending the threat are actions that change the life of the hero of the story.

The Universal Truth of Human Life

Heroic stories tell us the universal truth of human life. Life consists of one problem after another. Just as soon as you solve one problem, two more pop up, and you have to solve them too. Solve those problems, and more problems pop up. This is life. Problem after problem after problem.

Is Life a Beach?

Life is not about taking it easy, lounging on the beach somewhere, sipping margaritas while you watch the waves and the sunset.

Actually, you do need to have your moments on the beach, watching the waves and sunset—margaritas are optional—to recuperate, rest, and restore yourself, to prepare yourself for the next problem that comes your way.

However, the truth is that you would be bored out of your skull if you did nothing more than lie on the beach day after day with no challenges and no problems to solve.

Life really is about solving the problems that have a way of showing up, just as you are lounging on the beach, sipping your margarita, without a care in the world.

Suddenly, a palm branch falls on your head or you see a tidal wave heading toward the shore or someone runs up to you with a gun and demands all your money or your spouse says: "Honey, there's someone else. I want a divorce."

Whatever happens, you have an interruption in your vacation in a tropical paradise. You've got a threatening problem and the problem isn't going to go away by itself. You have to do something to solve it. But how?

Why You Need Stories

This is why you need heroic stories. Heroic stories not only teach you the truth that life is full of problems and threats, they teach you how to solve your problems.

They show you that ordinary people become heroes because they figure out how to solve the problems that suddenly intrude into their lives, forcing them to DO something.

The heroes start out afraid, confused, unskilled, and unsure of what they are going to do, but they persevere. They find a way to solve the problems or they die trying.

Heroic stories change your life because they teach you that you have the capacity to solve your problems.

This is why I really mean *stories* rather than "reframing" or "a made up excuse for something," or any other definition of story that doesn't grasp the essence of a heroic story as a narrative about efforts to solve an urgent problem in the face of a powerful threat.

Chapter 17

Who Are You in Your Life Story?

One of my favorite movies is *Joe Versus the Volcano*, a silly movie with bad reviews from the critics, which is also one of the profoundest movies I know. I'll return to this story later, but right now, I'll quote only one line from the movie.

Who Will Be a Hero for the Waponis?

Joe has been sent to the island of Waponi Woo to save the people by jumping into a volcano on their behalf to save the island from destruction. It's all about appeasing the volcano by offering up a willing human sacrifice to the volcano every hundred years.

There are two problems here. First, the Waponi people are in danger. The volcano is the threat. If the volcano is not appeased, the volcano will destroy the island, and all of the Waponis will die. The second problem is that no Waponi is willing to be the savior. After all, who really wants to jump into a volcano?

Joe becomes the hired savior for people who are not willing to save themselves. In this setting, Joe makes this statement: "I am my only hope for a hero."

Would These Words Change Your Life Story?

Who would you be in your life story if you faced every problem, every obstacle, every hurdle with these words:

> I am my only hope for a hero.

Such a mantra would begin to challenge the dominant lesson most of us have learned throughout our lives. Instead of learning to be heroes, we have learned to wait for someone to save us.

Did You Learn to Be Hero?

What is the dominant and enduring lesson that most of us learned as children? Isn't it that you are small and vulnerable and that you need to be saved from the dangers of the world? Didn't you learn that salvation is outside you, in the form of adults who save you from harm? Didn't you learn that you can't save yourself? Rather, you must hope for a hero to save you.

Salvation from harm is a powerful universal need of childhood, when vulnerable children really do need to be saved from dangers by adult saviors—especially when the adults in the child's world are the source of greatest danger.

Who Saves You?

What does the core claim of the Christian church teach you about being your only hope for a hero? Isn't it that Jesus is the savior who will save you because you cannot save yourself from your sinful nature? Did you learn to be a hero when you learned to hope that the hero Jesus will save you?

What does the primary claim of the Twelve Steps programs teach you about being your only hope for a hero? Isn't it that you cannot save yourself from your problem? Did you learn to be a hero when you learned that only the intervention of a higher power could save you from your addiction?

Did Stories Teach You to Be a Hero?

Meanwhile, all around you, weren't you immersed in a sea of stories about heroes who save the helpless? Did these stories teach you how to be a hero? Did they teach you how to save yourself? Or did they teach you to be helpless?

Families, churches, schools, books, TV, and movies all create an overwhelming environment that teaches you that your only hope for a hero lies outside of you. You learned to hope for a hero to save you from your problems.

Would This Question Change Your Life?

Before you object to any of these points, especially when it comes to Christian beliefs about salvation and the value of Twelve Steps programs to deal with addictions, I encourage you to simply ask this question:

> What would change in your life if you faced every problem with these words: I am my only hope for a hero?

We'll come back to this statement in Chapter 20. Joe wasn't really alone on his heroic journey. Heroes do need the help of others to accomplish their heroic tasks. For now, let it be enough to ponder the question.

And before we get too lost in the problems of life, let's consider the wonders of life itself.

Chapter 18

Amazement and Your Life Stories

Years ago, while I was in graduate school in Berkeley, California, I left a class one day to walk to the library. Bob was with me. Bob was a student in a class I was teaching. He was on a sabbatical year from working somewhere in Africa—I remember it as Namibia—to translate the Christian New Testament into a local dialect.

Rainbows in the Grass

As we walked out of the building, I saw that the lawn sprinklers were making small arcs of water about six inches high in the lawn. It was one of those magical moments when the sunlight hit the water at just the right angle. A dozen tiny rainbows glittered in the grass. It was a scene fit for fairy tale elves dancing Irish jigs under the rainbows.

I said, "Bob, look at the rainbows!"

Bob said, in a very matter of fact tone of voice, "It's the light shining on the water."

I was a bit surprised by his response and said something to the effect, "I know, but I really like rainbows."

Bob answered, "Some people do."

The Scent of Honeysuckles

I was silent for a few moments. By then, we were on the sidewalk, walking toward the library. We passed a row of honeysuckle bushes that were in full bloom. For days, I had been reveling in the sight and scent of the blossoms every time I walked by.

I was still a bit taken aback by Bob's indifference to the rainbows and his dismissive comment about how "some people" like rainbows. Clearly, Bob was not one of the "some people."

By the time we reached the honeysuckles, I wanted to find out if Bob was really that indifferent to little glimpses of beauty in the natural world, and so I said, "Bob, look at the honeysuckle blossoms."

Bob said, "Yes, those are honeysuckles."

At that moment, I stopped, grabbed a honeysuckle branch, and said, "Bob, come smell the honeysuckles."

He did but he was clearly not impressed.

We walked in silence the rest of the half block to the library. I have never forgotten my short walk with Bob, who could not be moved by the sight of rainbows or the scent of honeysuckles.

The Science and the Wonder

It's true. I'm one of the "some people" who like rainbows. Actually, I love rainbows. If the truth be told, I also do understand that rainbows are created by the refracting and reflecting of light onto water droplets that become prisms to separate the light into wavelengths of different colors. An undergraduate degree in chemistry and a few physics classes taught me enough about the physics of light to know that much. But having some understanding of the science of reflected and refracted light doesn't diminish the wonder that is a rainbow.

A State of Constant, Total Amazement

One of my favorite scenes in *Joe Versus the Volcano* occurs when Joe is on a boat in the ocean with Patricia. He is awed by the ocean and the stars. He says that it is all "unbelievable" to him.

At this point, Patricia says this:

My father says that almost the whole world is asleep. Everybody you know. Everybody you see. Everybody you talk to. He said that only a few people are awake and they live in a state of constant, total amazement.

It's so easy to get caught up in the problems of our lives. We can get so immersed in our troubles and our struggles, our hurts and our pains, our strivings to accomplish our big dreams and our failures and disappointments when we don't, that we don't notice that life itself is full of wonder.

That's why we also need moments of amazement. Those moments when tiny rainbows glitter in the grass and the scent of honeysuckle blossoms fills the air. In those moments of wonder, life becomes more than an endurance contest. Life itself becomes an experience of total amazement.

Chapter 19

Self-Actualized Individual or Hero?

Abraham Maslow's model of the *self-actualized individual* and the *hierarchy of needs* is an idea that is often uncritically accepted as an accurate description of how to be successful in life (Maslow).

Life Success of the Self-Actualized Competitor

The self-actualized individual is just that—an individual. In this vision of life success, life is about competition with others rather than collaboration. It's about separation rather than connection. It's about a solitary self rather than a person connected to some larger entity—a family, a tribe, a nation, a world, a galaxy. In other words, it's all about me, me, me.

Life Success of the Connected Hero

In contrast, the hero is always connected to others and the heroic journey is always about some benefit for others. The definition of life success for a hero is not just about personal achievement but about life success for some entity that extends beyond the individual. The self-actualized individual might become a success in life, but the successful hero also becomes a savior.

Chapter 20

You Are Not Alone

Do you feel alone in your struggles to change your life? We live in an era when it's possible for you to have social media friends by the thousands all the while you feel alone in your quest to accomplish your big dreams. The fundamental difference between Abraham Maslow's model of the self-actualized individual and Joseph Campbell's model of the hero comes down to this question: Can you really succeed in life alone?

Standing Alone

Maslow's pyramid is a lonely climb to the top. The model emphasizes individual achievement without acknowledging the role of others who helped the self-actualized individual reach the top of the success pyramid

In contrast, the great paradox of the hero's journey model is that the hero has mentors, friends, and companions on the journey but that the hero has to accomplish the final task alone. Hero's journey stories are not about "self-made men pulling themselves up by their bootstraps." They are stories about people on a mission to solve a problem. They cannot do it alone.

At the final point of the hero's journey, the hero is much like the self-actualized individual on the top of the pyramid. The hero stands alone just as the self actualized individual stands alone.

When the self-actualized individual stands alone at the top of the pyramid, it's a sign of personal success. When the hero stands alone, the hero must face the ultimate test that will determine whether or not the hero succeeds in accomplishing the heroic task.

Frodo, the Ring, and the Fire

One of the most obvious examples of the paradox between doing it alone and having help along the way is the hobbit, Frodo, in *The Lord of the Rings* trilogy. Frodo's heroic mission is to take the Ring of Power to Mount Doom where he will destroy the ring by throwing it into the fire. This is Frodo's heroic task. No one can do it for him. He must face the final test alone.

But for Frodo to get to Mount Doom, he needs help from mentors, friends, and companions, in the form of humans, wizards, elves, a dwarf, and other hobbits. He especially needs the help of his steadfast companion Sam. Frodo couldn't get to Mount Doom without Sam, but Sam cannot throw the ring into the fire. Only Frodo can accomplish Frodo's heroic task.

The Whole Truth about Life Success

This is the primary reason why Maslow's model of the self actualized individual doesn't tell the whole truth about life success. No one ever gets to the top alone. Everyone needs help along the way.

In contrast to Maslow's do-it-yourself model, the model of the hero journey tells you the encouraging truth about life success. You are not alone when you set out on your own heroic journey to change your life and the lives of others. You will have help along the way. Mentors. Friends. Companions. And if you are truly blessed, you will have your own version of Sam — the one who goes with you all the way.

Part 5

What Do Your Life Stories Cost?

Originally Published February 14-18, 2011

KalindaRoseStevenson.com

Chapter 21

Do You Sell Your Soul for Money?

How many of your life stories are money stories about what you will or will not do for money? As a story, *Joe Versus the Volcano*, is an extended parable about what people will do for money. The story shows people sleepwalking through their lives, half dead, for the sake of their jobs.

Tom Hanks is Joe Banks. The first truths that we learn about him are that he has a lousy job and that he doesn't feel well. One of his first lines of dialogue in the movie is, "I am losing my sole." He points to his shoe, but the remark makes clear that the lousy job is costing him his soul. We also discover that the job is costing him his health.

Nobody Feels Good

Everyone at Joe's job is sick and looks half dead. The secretary needs an inhaler to breathe and is afraid of death, even though she is already half dead. Joe never feels good and spends much of his time and money visiting doctors. His thoroughly reprehensible and miserable boss, Mr. Waturi, makes the statement:

> Nobody feels good. After childhood, it's a fact of life. But I don't let it bother me. I don't let it interfere with my job.

Joe's doctor tells Joe that he is dying with a mysterious illness and has exactly six months to live. The diagnosis is a lie, but Joe doesn't know that.

Joe returns to his miserable windowless, basement office lit by buzzing fluorescent lights. He realizes that he has sold his soul and sacrificed his life for a job paying him three hundred dollars a week. Joe quits his job, and goes home to wait to die.

How Much Does It Cost to Buy a Life?

The next day, the ultra-rich Mr. Granamore shows up and makes Joe an offer. If Joe will go to a tiny island in the South Pacific and jump into a volcano to appease the angry volcano, Mr. Granamore will get rights to a rare mineral called *boobaroo*.

What's the price that Mr. Granamore will pay for Joe's life? A stack of credit cards, a night on the town, a first-class airplane flight to Los Angeles, and an ocean voyage on his sailboat, the Tweedle-Dee.

Despite the preposterous plot and some bad acting, the movie raises profound questions about life choices and what people will do for money.

Chapter 22

Trading the Priceless for Orange Soda

Did you ever see the ads by the credit card company about the difference between the things you can buy with your credit card and the experiences that are priceless? The purpose of the ads is to persuade you that things with a price tag are worth buying because those things can create priceless experiences.

Joe Versus the Volcano is about the opposite effect. It's a money story about the high cost of trading the priceless for something that comes with a price tag.

What People Do for Money

Traditional stories are full of examples of people who traded the priceless for a price. What is the price tag of any life? What is the tradeoff between honor and money?

Two familiar examples from the Bible are the stories of Esau and Judas. Esau traded his birthright as the first-born son for a bowl of lentils. How much is a bowl of lentils worth? You can put a price tag on that. You cannot put a price tag on your status as the first-born son in a patriarchal society:

> Once when Jacob was cooking a stew, Esau came in from the field, and he was famished. Esau said to Jacob, "Let me eat some of that red stuff, for I am famished!" (Therefore he was called Edom.) Jacob said, "First sell me your birthright." Esau said, "I am about to die; of what use is a birthright to me?" Jacob said, "Swear to me first." So he swore to him, and sold his birthright to Jacob. Then Jacob gave Esau bread and lentil stew, and he ate and drank, and rose and went his way. Thus Esau despised his birthright (NRSV 25:29-34).

In the best known example of all, Judas betrayed Jesus for thirty pieces of silver:

> Then one of the twelve, who was called Judas Iscariot, went to the chief priests and said, "What will you give me if I betray him to you?" They paid him thirty pieces of silver. And from that moment he began to look for an opportunity to betray him. (NRSV 26:14-16).

Neither of these stories ends well. Esau lost both his birthright as the first-born and his father's blessing

(Genesis 27:30-41) and Judas gave back the money and then hanged himself (Matthew 27:3-5).

A Money Story about Tradeoffs

If you can get past the over-the-top silly stuff in *Joe Versus the Volcano*, particularly about orange soda guzzling Polynesians, who roll out a huge red carpet on a wheel, while eating grapes on a South Pacific atoll that has never seen a grapevine, as they mock their hired hero with preposterous antics, all the while singing and dancing a Hebrew hora, you will see a money story about people who have made tradeoffs of the priceless in exchange for something with a price tag.

What People Do For Money

How much is health worth? Joe trades his health for three hundred dollars a week.

How much is a life worth? Mr. Granamore is willing to trade Joe's life for a rare mineral boobaroo that comes with a high price tag.

How much is self-respect worth? Angelica trades her self-respect for Daddy's money and all the things that Daddy's money can buy.

How much is the preservation of your island and the lives of your people worth? The Waponis are willing to trade the well-being of their people for orange soda.

These are the tradeoffs between things with a price and things that are truly priceless in the movie.

Some know they have done it. Some haven't. But all pay a high price for trading the priceless for something with a price tag.

Chapter 23

Soul Sick

What if the best way to change your life is to first become *soul sick*? *Joe Versus the Volcano* is a money story about soul sickness. Soul sickness is a condition brought on by selling out your authentic self for some gain. It can be money. It can be fame. It can be popularity. It can be security. Whatever it is, the price is too high.

Your Authentic Self Becomes Soul Sick

Above all, soul sickness is a state of awareness. You become soul sick when you become aware that you have compromised your true self—your authentic self—for something that is not worth the tradeoff.

Patricia, played by Meg Ryan, is the character in the story with the most self-awareness. She is the one who calls herself soul sick.

Would You Sell Your Soul for the TweedleDee?

In Patricia's case, she knows she is soul sick because she made a deal with her father. She had promised herself that she would never take anything from her father. But he offered her the one thing she wanted—the yacht named TweedleDee—and she made the deal. She would get the boat if she agreed to transport Joe to Waponi Woo.

Patricia is soul sick because she recognizes that she had a price and would sell her soul for that price.

Patricia is both mentor and companion on Joe's hero's journey about his growing awareness that he too is soul sick because he sold his soul for three hundred dollars per week.

The Brain Cloud Diagnosis

At the beginning of the story, Joe is aware only that he is sick. He has some awareness that he is losing his sole/soul, but he has not yet figured out the connection between his health problems and the loss of his authentic self. He looks for answers from doctors and medical tests, but he is not yet aware that the real solution lies only within himself.

The starting point of Joe's hero's journey comes in the form of a medical diagnosis. Joe has a "brain cloud." A brain cloud is a rare medical condition, which has no symptoms and no medical treatment, which will cause Joe's brain to fail abruptly in six months.

The Start of Joe's Hero's Journey

This diagnosis is the interruption in Joe's ordinary world that begins his hero's journey. For the first time, Joe becomes aware of the price he has paid to earn three hundred dollars each week. He realizes that he has sold his soul to work in a miserable job, doing work with no value, with despicable people, in working conditions that rob people of their health. With this first awareness of the high cost of his soul sickness, Joe quits the job.

Three Life Choices to Change Your Life

The three women characters in the movie—each played by Meg Ryan—have all sold their souls, but have different levels of awareness and willingness to do anything about it.

DeeDee, who is also stuck in the same office as Joe, is sick, but not yet soul sick. She has no apparent self-awareness that she is trading her authentic life for a paycheck. She is too afraid to lose her job to change her life.

Patricia's half-sister, Angelica, is also soul sick. She is aware that she has traded her authentic self to live on her father's money, but she is unwilling to do the one thing she knows would set her free from her soul sickness—leave Los Angeles and stop taking her father's money.

Patricia is the only one who is willing to go on the hero's journey with Joe. On the journey, she also heals her own soul sickness.

Soul Sick to Save Your Authentic Self

The deep truth of this money story is that the way to change your life is to first become soul sick, by seeing clearly how much it has cost to you to sell your soul for something that was not worth the price.

Although soul sickness is painful, it can often be a necessary experience in your hero's journey to change your life.

Chapter 24

Live It Well

As a character in the hero's journey story of *Joe Versus the Volcano*, Dr. Ellison is a paradoxical mentor for Joe's hero's journey.

A Paradoxical Mentor

As a mentor, Dr. Ellison is both a liar and a truth teller. He identifies the brain cloud as the threat facing Joe. He also gives Joe an essential gift for his hero's journey to find his lost soul.

Dr. Ellison's money story is that he sold his soul to Mr. Granamore and is willing to lie to Joe with a made-up diagnosis about a "brain cloud." But the story is not about Dr. Ellison and the tradeoffs he made to be Mr. Granamore's lackey, to be willing to trade his integrity as a physician for the benefits of being Mr. Granamore's private—and presumably well-paid—doctor.

Why Mr. Granamore's private doctor sees Joe as a patient is a bit inconsistent with the storyline, but the flaw in the story allows Joe to get the medical diagnosis that is necessary for the story and the invitation by Mr. Granamore to be the savior of the Waponis.

The Threat and the Gift

On one side of the paradox, Dr. Ellison as a liar provides the diagnosis that gives Joe the reason to accept Mr. Granamore's deal to jump into the volcano so that Mr. Granamore can get his boobaroo. Without the lie, Joe would never have started the journey to Waponi Woo, which is another way of stating that he would not have started on his life changing hero's journey.

On the other side of the paradox, Dr. Ellison as the truth teller provides the gift that gives Joe the essential reason to be heroic. When Joe believes that he is going to die, he makes a life changing decision about how he will die.

The Life Changing Paradox

The paradox of the diagnosis is that the lie about Joe's imminent death from an incurable "brain cloud" provides the foundation for Joe to reclaim his authentic life.

The brain cloud diagnosis is a stark reminder that Joe's time is limited. The story brings to the surface the fact of human mortality and that we, as human beings, have choices about how we live and how we die.

The Choice to Live It Well

When Joe realizes that he has only six months left to live, he asks Dr. Ellison this question: What am I going to do?

Dr. Ellison then speaks these words of wisdom:

> You have some time left, Mr. Banks. You have some life left. My advice is to you is, live it well.

This is the core idea of *Joe Versus the Volcano*. These words force Joe to consider how he will live and how he will die. These words are the gift that motivates Joe's journey and shapes his decisions. He decides that he will live the rest of his life well. In Joe's case, this means that he will jump into a volcano on Waponi Woo so that he can die a hero.

Soul Sick over Lost Time

Although Joe accepts the truth of his own impending death without much difficulty, Joe experiences his own soul sickness when he recognizes how much of his life he wasted.

Soul sickness is not just the sense that Joe traded his authentic self for three hundred dollars a week, but that he wasted his precious life by doing it. When Joe realizes that he has only six months left to live, he quits his job because he is unwilling to spend another minute doing the job he hates.

Life Changing Questions

The core idea of *Joe Versus the Volcano* applies to all of us. You don't need a diagnosis of six months to live to ask questions about your life.

What do you do about time you can never get back? About mistakes you have made? About bad choices? About all of the things you planned to do and never got done? About the time you didn't spend with the people you love? And more significantly, what do you do with the time you have left?

The wisdom lying on the surface of this movie applies to all of us. No matter how young or old you are right now, no matter what your current situation, whatever your life story up to this point, these words are profoundly relevant:

You have some time left. You have some life left. My advice is, use it well.

Chapter 25

What Do You Have to Change?

What do you have to change to be your authentic self? The hero's journey is not about how you have to change your life so that you become something you never were before. It's about becoming who you truly are or have the potential to become.

In *Joe Versus the Volcano*, the hero in Joe—Joe's authentic self—had gone into hiding because Joe was afraid.

How Joe Became Afraid

We find out in the session with Dr. Ellison that Joe had worked in the fire department. He left the fire department because he didn't feel good. Dr. Ellison diagnoses Joe's problem this way:

> Dr. Ellison: "My guess is that your experiences in the fire department were extremely traumatic. You experienced the imminent possibility of death several times?"
>
> Joe: "Yeah."

> Dr. Ellison: "The cumulative anxiety with those brushes with death left you habitually fearful about your physical person."

This little scene tells us two facts about Joe. He used to be a fireman. We also know that he got very scared.

Trying to Find the Hero

After Joe quits his job, he gets a visit from Mr. Granamore. Mr. Granamore peers into Joe's eyes and says:

> Mr. Granamore: "I'm trying to find the hero in there."
>
> Joe: "What do you mean?"
>
> Mr. Granamore: "You dragged two kids down a six story burning staircase. Now that's brave. Then you went back for the third kid. That was heroic. Come on now. You're a hero."
>
> Joe: "Well, that was a long time ago."
>
> Mr. Granamore: "Yes, it was."

And this is the real truth about Joe before he started to feel bad all the time. He had been a hero, a long time ago, before he became afraid.

Why did Mr. Granamore choose Joe for his business proposition? He was looking for a hero. He needed someone willing to jump into a volcano to save the Waponis from the angry fire god in the volcano. Who would be better for the job than a man who had a history of jumping into burning burnings to save people?

Why Would I Jump into a Volcano?

Mr. Granamore, for his own selfish purposes, is appealing to Joe to become the hero Joe was before he became afraid. The hero in Joe hadn't really gone away. He had gone into hiding in the bowels of a dismal factory—a factory that is the "Home of the Rectal Probe."

If Mr. Granamore is going to get the boobaroo for his superconductors, he has to sell Joe on the idea of jumping into a volcano.

Joe asks an obvious question: "Why would I jump into a volcano?"

In an inspired sales pitch, Mr. Granamore gives Joe a renewed vision of his authentic self. He answers Joe's question by appealing to Joe's sense of his true self, the self that has been hiding in the depths of the dismal factory and his dingy apartment:

> Because of your exploits in the fire department, I think you've got the courage. All I know is that when you're

making those calls you're up in the high country. From your doctor you know you're on your way out anyway. You haven't got any money. I checked.

Do you want to wait it out here in this apartment? Sounds kinda grim to me. Not the way I'd want to go. I tell you that. Live like a king, die like a man. That's what I say. Waddya say?

Joe answers simply: "All right, I'll do it."

Is There More to the Story?

From one perspective, *Joe Versus the Volcano* is a story about the need to do what you are most afraid to do. About summoning up your courage and taking leaps of faith. What could be a better symbol of doing what you fear than choosing to jump into a volcano?

This is the most obvious conclusion, but there is something even more significant going on in this story than telling you to do the thing you're most of afraid of doing.

In this story, Joe is not really afraid to jump. Joe has a history of courage and a history of leaping into burning buildings to save people. After Joe makes his decision to go to Waponi Woo to die a hero, he never backs down from the decision.

Joe is resolute, even when he falls in love with Patricia. He will die as the hero that he was before he became afraid.

Becoming Your Authentic Self

This is the most essential truth about *Joe Versus the Volcano*. The hero's journey is not about changing yourself into someone you aren't, but becoming who you truly are—your authentic self.

Part 6

Stories on

Your Life Storywheel

Originally Published February 7-11, 2011

KalindaRoseStevenson.com

Chapter 26

Going in Circles on Your Life Storywheel

Life is about going in circles. Movement in life is made up of circles going in circles within circles within circles. It's the moon orbiting the earth, which is orbiting the sun, which is orbiting within the galaxy. It's the "wheels within wheels" in the vision of the prophet Ezekiel (Ezekiel 1:16). It's the small gears rotating around bigger gears in your analog watch.

James Bonnet, in *Stealing Fire from the Gods*, uses the model of the storywheel to locate every human story somewhere on the ongoing cycle of ascents and descents:

> Storywheel: A model that brings all the different types of great story together into one grand design. Viewed this way, all of the cycles of change and growth we experience from birth to death are revealed, and it becomes apparent that the purpose of great stories is to guide us to higher states of being (Bonnet 260).

Your life story is made up of small storywheels within larger storywheels within the whole storywheel of your life.

At the same time, good stories are also linear. The hero on a hero's journey has one mission and must focus on that objective to accomplish that mission. This means that stories require single-minded focus in one direction:

> Frodo must get the Ring of Power to Mount Doom in *The Lord of the Rings*.

> Indiana Jones must find the lost Ark of the Covenant in *Raiders of the Lost Ark*.

> Neo must destroy Mr. Smith in *Matrix*.

Your Storywheel

The value of the storywheel model is that it tells the truth that our lives are never lived in a straight line. We actually live our lives going in circles, with ups and downs, with ascents and descents, with good times and bad times.

Real human life stories are more complicated than a single story located somewhere on a storywheel. Your life story is not just one story. It is made up of lots of stories, all rotating within the whole of your life story. Not one of these life stories follows a straight line.

Spinning Plates

For most of us, life looks more like the circus act with the spinning plates. The juggler manages to keep all the plates spinning without letting any of them crash to the ground. The rest of us don't do so well with the spinning plates that represent the multitude of simultaneous story cycles going on in our lives at any given moment. Most of us know all too well the sound of crashing plates.

This means that you are attempting to change your life all the while you are going around in circles on a storywheel that is made up of multiple storywheels.

The Good News

Does this sound discouraging to you? All of this around and around, up and down, good times and bad? Do you wish that you could live in a straight line, to get from here to there without so many ups and downs on the way?

When you think about the whole of your life as a life story lived on a storywheel made up of multitudes of smaller storywheels, all of this movement is actually encouraging news.

Life on your own storywheel means that if you are down, you don't have to stay down. If you don't have what you truly desire in life, you can change your life by doing something to change it. You aren't stuck where you are. The storywheel that is your life is still going in circles.

Chapter 27

Change Your Life by Going in a Straight Line

Seeing your life story as a storywheel that contains multiple storywheels emphasizes the cycles of our lives, the ups and the downs, the ascents and the descents as part of every life story. At the same time, your life story requires straight lines in any effort to accomplish specific goals.

Success in life requires focus. What is focus? In physics, *focus* is the "point at which rays of light, heat, or other radiation, meet after being refracted or reflected" (Dictionary.com, *focus*). Focus is about the central point of your attention. Focus is about straight lines to get from here to there.

So here is the challenge for us mere mortals who inhabit a spinning ball called Earth. If you want to get what you want in life, you need to find a way to focus your attention in a straight line in a universe of cyclical motions.

The Apollo 13 Moon Mission

There is no better example of a story that demonstrates the interplay of lines and circles in accomplishing some goal than *Apollo 13*, a movie based on the story of a manned lunar mission that went terribly wrong.

You can read NASA's own record of the Apollo 13 mission (NASA).

Let's begin with the initial objective. NASA's goal was to launch a manned spaceship with the specific goal of landing at a particular location on the Moon—the Fra Mauro site. This is the straight line component of the project. Get to the Moon in as straight a line as possible.

A Linear Objective in a World Going in Circles

Notice that it is "as straight a line as possible." A mission to the Moon is a dramatic example of a linear objective in a world going in circles.

Accomplishing the objective of the mission involves propelling a spaceship into space from one moving ball so that it can land on a smaller moving ball, then return from the smaller moving ball to land back on the bigger moving ball.

A moon mission is all about the orbits and trajectories of moving bodies:

> It means knowing how both Earth and the Moon change.
>
> It means knowing how to use the momentum of the Moon in its orbit.
>
> It means knowing the forces of attraction between two orbiting bodies in space.
>
> It means knowing about forces of gravity at work on each orbiting body.

NASA needed to know all of this, and much more, to plot the straightest possible line to the Moon.

Intersection of Lines and Circles

All stories demonstrate this kind of interplay between straight lines and circles, including your own life story.

If you are on a moon mission, you know that you have to pay attention to orbits, trajectories, and momentum to find the straightest line possible to your target.

For the rest of us, the intersection of lines and circles in our life stories is nowhere nearly as obvious or dramatic as it is on a moon mission. That doesn't make the interplay of lines and circles any less real.

If you want to change your life by transforming your life story, you will need to understand how to focus on a specific target in a world going in circles.

Chapter 28

Events Transpire to Get You Home

One of the most powerful themes of *Apollo 13* is that the astronauts could not get home without the help of thousands of people and the heartfelt concern of millions more. These words from *Apollo 13* capture the essence of the story:

> You never know what events are going to transpire to get you home.

Apollo 13 is a story about three men in a crippled spacecraft, thousands of miles from Earth, without power, without navigation, without heat, without sleep, without food, without any reasonable expectation that they would survive. Despite all of this, they got home.

In one of the first scenes of the movie, we hear the voice of Tom Hanks as Jim Lovell before we see him:

> The astronaut is only the most visible of a very large team and all of us, right down to the guy sweeping the floor, are honored to a part of it (Hanks, *Apollo 13*).

NASA's Finest Hour

In his commentary, Director Ron Howard says that as many as five thousand people in NASA and private industries worked relentlessly to find a way to get the astronauts back home after the catastrophe. All of these efforts became NASA's "finest hour" because the people working on the ground did the impossible. They brought the astronauts back alive.

But beyond finding the solutions to the technical problems—which is a compelling story in itself—there is something else compelling about this story.

Humanity's Finest Hour

Getting the astronauts home was not just NASA's finest hour, but one of humanity's finest hours. It was one of those rare moments in human history when we transcend our differences and collectively intend the best for others.

Have there ever been human beings more isolated from the rest of humanity than the three men trapped in a crippled spacecraft on a path around the dark side of the moon? And yet, their plight connected them with the world.

Connected by Good Will

We live in such a polarized world, so often lacking in compassion and concern, so full of reminders of what separates us from each other.

Apollo 13 is a vision of what happens when the people of Earth combine to have good will toward others. It portrays one of those rare moments when human beings realize that we are all connected to each other, that we all share the same desire to live and to find our way to get home.

In the case of the Apollo 13 astronauts, people throughout the world held their collective breath and hoped, against all hope, that these men would get home again.

Involved In Humankind

John Donne captured the essence of this connectedness in some of the best-known words in the English language:

> No man is an island,
> Entire of itself.
> Each is a piece of the continent,
> A part of the main.
> If a clod be washed away by the sea,

> Europe is the less.
>
> As well as if a promontory were.
>
> As well as if a manor of thine own
>
> Or of thine friend's were.
>
> Each man's death diminishes me,
>
> For I am involved in mankind.
>
> Therefore, send not to know
>
> For whom the bell tolls,
>
> It tolls for thee (Donne).

As a story with the power to change your life, *Apollo 13* tells a deep truth about getting help when you need to find your way home.

Chapter 29

Alone on Your Own Dark Side of the Moon

Getting help with problems is one thing if you are a celebrity. A movie such as *Apollo 13* evokes the best in us, the sense of being connected. It's a triumph of human determination and a shining moment of unified good will and compassion for the plight of three men stranded in space.

But what about the other side of the story? The astronauts got home from the dark side of the moon because they were celebrities. As celebrities, they got help from thousands of people working for their benefit. The story also unintentionally draws a dramatic contrast between the lives of celebrities and the lives of the rest of us.

No Help with Your Problems

What if you are not a celebrity? What if you feel that you are living your life on your own metaphorical dark side of the moon. A place of isolation. You feel cut off from communication. Cut off from help. Cut off anyone who cares very much whether you live or die. A place where no one is going to help you with problems.

Feeling Alone

We live in lonely times. We can connect with people all over the world, at the speed of electrons. At the same time, we live in an era of great loneliness for many people who feel isolated. It's one of the great disconnects of our era that the more we are connected by technology and social media, the less real contact we have with living, breathing people.

Especially now, especially when millions of people are facing problems they cannot solve alone. Facing foreclosure or already homeless. Facing bankruptcy or already bankrupt. Facing a mountain of debt. Unable to find a job. Unable to pay the bills. In these hard economic times, millions have lost their homes, their jobs, their savings, their hope for the future. With such problems, many people feel profoundly alone. Maybe even you.

Who Helps You?

Who helps you with your problems when you are going through your own catastrophe on your own very lonely, and very private, dark side of the moon? Where are the thousands of people working relentlessly to help you find your way back home? Where are the millions of people who care what happens to you? Who is going to help you with your problems?

What Is Your Current Reality?

At this point, I'm not going to switch focus to metaphysics, to claim that we are all connected, that all of our separation is illusory. I don't mean to challenge the validity of such metaphysical claims. Such metaphysical claims might be true but they don't help much if you can't pay the mortgage or put food on the table.

Who Helps You Right Now?

Here is a perspective on current reality. Have you ever thought about how many thousands, maybe even millions, of people work behind the scenes to make your life possible?

Despite all of the claims from people who say they want freedom and liberty from any sort of interference in their lives, we all benefit from the help of other people.

Look around you. Look at what you have. Look at what other people have provided for you. The food that people grow. The roads that people pave. The water that is pumped to your home. The sewer systems. The police departments. The fire departments. The schools that taught you to read.

Everything you have, even when you are struggling to survive in a lonely world, is the direct result of what other people have done for you.

It's Not a Miracle

Consider the extraordinary technology of computers. Have you ever considered how much a computer is the product of thousands of years of human creativity, human productivity, human initiative? None of this is miraculous. We have this technology because human beings created it.

In *Apollo 13,* on the night that Neil Armstrong first walks on the moon, Tom Hanks as Jim Lovell makes this statement about going to the moon:

> It's not a miracle. We just decided to go (Hanks, *Apollo 13*).

And so, whatever problems you are facing right now in your life, as difficult as they are, the truth of *Apollo 13* is the truth for you too. You are already getting help from untold millions of human beings, working throughout the generations of human history to provide what you have.

Chapter 30

Success after Your Big Dream Dies

Apollo 13 is also a story about the death of a dream. As the astronaut who had already spent more time in space than any of the other astronauts, Jim Lovell had one remaining dream. He wanted to walk on the Moon. His dream died when the explosion turned the moon mission into a rescue mission.

The Successful Failure of Apollo 13

In the closing monologue, Tom Hanks as Jim Lovell says:

> Our mission was called a successful failure in that we returned safely but never made it to the Moon. In the following months, it was determined that a damaged coil, built inside the oxygen tank, sparked during our cryostir and caused the explosion that crippled the Odyssey. It was a minor defect that occurred two years before I was named the flight's commander.
>
> ...
>
> As for me, the seven extraordinary days of Apollo 13 were my last in space. I watched other men walk on the

moon and return safely, all from the confines of Mission Control and our house in Houston.

I sometimes catch myself looking up at the Moon, remembering the changes of fortune in our long voyage, thinking of the thousands of people who worked to bring the three of us home.

I look up at the Moon and I wonder, when will we be going back and who will that be (Hanks, *Apollo 13*).

The Death of the Big Dream

Apollo 13 was a success for one reason. The crew and ground control recognized that the goal of landing on the Moon was impossible. They succeeded only because they gave up on their original goal and changed their mission. They succeeded because they recognized the death of the big dream.

Persistence, No Matter What?

In the context of *Apollo 13*, I pose this question: What if many of us fail because we are unwilling to quit when the big dream is already dead?

Just raising this question runs counter to so much of the accepted dogma of success literature, which emphasizes that success in life depends on persistence, no matter what.

The Habit Of Quitting

Consider this anecdote from the "Bible" of success literature, *Think and Grow Rich,* by Napoleon Hill.

Hill precedes the story with this statement:

> One of the most common causes of failure is the habit of quitting when one is overtaken by temporary defeat (Hill 20).

Hill goes on to tell the story of a man who discovered a rich vein of ore. The man raised money for machinery to mine the ore. After mining some of the gold, the miners discovered that the vein of gold stopped.

> The vein of gold had disappeared! They had come to the end of the rainbow, and the pot of gold was no longer there. They drilled on, desperately trying to pick up the vein again—all to no avail. Finally, they decided to quit (Hill 20).

Hill tells the rest of the story. The man and his partner sold the mine to a "junk man" for a few hundred dollars.

The junk man consulted experts and found out about fault lines. With expert guidance, the junk man found the vein of gold just three feet from where the Darbys had stopped drilling.

> The junk man took millions of dollars in ore from the mine because he knew enough to seek expert counsel before giving up (Hill 21).

Then Hill makes this point about many of the successful men he interviewed:

> More than five hundred of the most successful men this country has ever known told the author that their greatest success came just one step beyond the point at which defeat had overtaken them. Failure is a trickster with a keen sense of irony and cunning. It takes great delight in tripping one when success is most within reach (Hill 21-22).

Does Life Success Mean You Never Quit?

It is only one tiny step from such a story to the idea that quitting is *always* a sign of failure:

> Finally, they decided to *quit* (Hill 20).

This phrase, with the word quit in italics in the Plume Book version, screams out a judgment that the decision to quit mining the gold is incomprehensible. How could they quit? Can you imagine? They decided to quit! What losers! This type of thinking leads to such simplistic aphorisms as:

> Winners never quit and quitters never win.

The Life Success Perspective of Apollo 13

Apollo 13 shows another perspective on quitting. Sometimes, it really is impossible to do what you set out to do. Sometimes, the only path to success is to quit and make another plan.

If you read Hill's story carefully, you will see that Hill refers to quitting in the face of "temporary defeat" and the problem of quitting before seeking expert counsel.

I expect that Napoleon Hill would agree completely that the explosion in the oxygen tank that crippled Apollo 13 was more than a "temporary defeat." And the crew of Apollo 13 certainly had expert counsel telling them that it was impossible to complete their mission.

Temporary or Permanent Defeat

How can you tell the difference between temporary defeat and permanent defeat? How do you know when to persist and when to change direction?

Robert Fritz claims in *The Path of Least Resistance* that the primary reason most people do not create their dreams is because of inaccurate assessment of current reality. In order to create what you choose to create, you need to know what currently exists (Fritz 51).

In the case of Apollo 13, the decision to quit was obvious. The current reality of Apollo 13 was that a decision to continue toward the Moon, to attempt to land on the Moon, no matter what, would have been a death sentence for the crew.

If you're not in a crippled spacecraft two hundred thousand miles from Earth, it can be harder to figure out the difference between temporary defeat and permanent defeat.

The important point is to ask the question: Do you continue with your plan or are you persisting in pursuit of a dream that is already dead?

Part 7

Creating Your Life Stories

Originally Published January 31-February 4, 2011

KalindaRoseStevenson.com

Part 7

Creating a Healthier You

Chapter 31

Be a Storyteller to Transform Your Life Story

A story is about problems. Up to this point, stories are set in motion by flat tire events. A flat tire event is some unexpected problem that you cannot ignore. The flat tire forces you to do something to solve the problem.

Hero's Journey Stories

The flat tire event is the foundation of hero journey stories. Something happens in the hero's ordinary world that forces the hero on a journey to solve the problem.

The key point here is that the hero does not choose the journey any more than you choose to have a flat tire on your way to work. Something or someone intrudes into the hero's ordinary world and creates an urgent problem that must be solved. The hero is the one who sets out—however reluctantly—to solve the problem. Anyone who undertakes the heroic journey and solves the problem is permanently changed by the journey.

This model of a hero's journey contains enormous power to change your life. However as a method for transforming your life, the model has a significant flaw. You are forced to change your life because of some outer circumstances. The flat tire event happens to you. You didn't plan it. You didn't choose the task. You didn't choose the journey. You do it because you feel compelled to do it.

Be the Storyteller of Your Life Story

The process to change your life by changing your stories makes one powerful change to the model of the hero's journey. Instead of waiting for flat tire events to change your life, you become the storyteller who creates your own hero's journey.

Stories are created by storytellers. The storyteller is the one who creates the problem, creates the characters, creates the obstacles, creates the outcome. When you create your own story, you are the one who has choices about every aspect of your story.

The Storyteller Must Be Ruthless

I consider myself very much a beginner in the art and craft of creating a good story. I have learned much from books and classes on stories and screenwriting. I have even written a few stories and drafts of screenplays myself. I know they're not very good stories and I don't expect Hollywood to come calling. I also know that I have loved the creative process of writing them, of creating characters and challenges, and discovering how the characters took on lives of their own as unexpected events occurred in their lives.

But even though I have much to learn about telling stories, I understand this much: the storyteller needs to be ruthless with the hero.

Although marketers and advertisers might promise that your life will be filled with riches, fame, romance, and perfect health if you buy whatever product they are selling, a good storyteller will make the hero's life hard. The harder the better.

The adversary will not be a paper tiger but a formidable foe. The obstacles will be not be molehills but mountains. The hero will not be perfect but will bumble forward, making mistake after mistake. The task will not be child's play but a difficult challenge.

Yet despite all of these obstacles, the hero will persevere, despite loss and grief and sadness and injury and betrayal, to solve the problem and complete the journey.

At the same time, the task must be something that is possible, something that is within the range of human capacity, something that a resolute, determined, persevering hero can accomplish.

The Storyteller's Challenge

It's a real challenge—at least I have found it to be—to write such a story. If you learn to love the characters you create in your story, the last thing you want to do is to make them suffer, struggle, and fail along the way. The temptation is to make the journey easy and the foes into pushovers.

Yet ruthlessness is exactly what a story about life change requires. No one has to undergo any sort of transformation if life is a bed of roses.

Become the Storyteller of Your Own Life Story

What does all of this mean to you as a process to transform your own life story? It means that you don't let flat tire events define your life. You become your own storyteller.

You can be the one who creates the hero's journey you will undertake. You can be the one who defines the purpose of the journey. You can change your life story because you create a new story.

This freedom to be the storyteller of your own life story means that you have the same responsibility as any storyteller who wants to tell good stories. You need to tell the truth about what it would take to change your life by transforming your life story.

Chapter 32

Be the Creator of Your Life Story

The critical distinction between hero's journey stories and changing your life with stories is that you can choose to become your own storyteller.

Problem Solving or Creating?

The distinction that can do more to change your life than any other single idea is the difference between problem solving and creating. I owe my own awareness of this distinction to the book by Robert Fritz, *The Path of Least Resistance: Learning to Become the Creative Force in Your Own Life*. Here's the difference:

> There is a profound difference between problem solving and creating. Problem solving is taking action to have something go away—the problem. Creating is taking action to have something come into being—the creation (Fritz 31).

I'm not exaggerating when I tell you that this distinction is one of the most important ideas I have ever learned.

One Problem after Another

Consider how much of your life story is defined by your problems, by reacting to circumstances, by trying to fix things that don't work. How much time and effort do you expend on trying to get rid of what you don't want in your life? How much of your life is about flat tire events, about "putting out fires," about crises, calamities, and catastrophes?

And then, stop and consider: How much of your life energy—your time, your effort, your money, your skills, your imagination—do you spend to create what you actually desire to have, to be, or do in your life?

In starkest terms, the difference between problem solving and creating is the difference between hate and love. How much of your life is about making what you hate go away? How much of your life is about causing what you love to come into existence?

The Limits of the Hero's Journey Story Model

On this point, the hero journey story model can take you only so far. Hero's journey stories are about the flat tire events, the crises, the urgent problems that cannot be ignored. Reluctant heroes are forced to do something because the problem must be solved. That's how it is in hero journey stories.

In contrast to hero's journeys, where the hero acts to solve the problem, most of us don't take action unless we have to. Our problems have to be big enough to overcome our own inertia. If the house catches fire, we'll get moving to get out of the house. Otherwise, it's easier to pop in a DVD, lie back in the La-Z-Boy, and watch a movie—my own personal favorite diversion from taking creative action.

This is why storytellers need to find a way to get someone to budge, to hit the road on the hero's journey to solve the problem. Aliens start to blow up the planet and you had better head for the hills. Your son is kidnapped and you just got a ransom note. You're on a ship that hits an iceberg. Enemy forces attack at dawn and destroy the fleet. Evil forces threaten life itself. These are all serious enough to get even the most reluctant among us decide to do something.

For most of us, the problem has to be big enough, urgent enough, and critical enough before we take action to solve the problem. At that point the motive is all about making the unwanted problem go away.

Create Your Own Story to Change Your Life

Here's the critical point. When you are the storyteller of your own life, you don't have to define your life by your problems. You have the freedom to define your life by what you would love to create.

Instead of a heroic journey to make something you hate go away, you can undertake a heroic journey to cause what you love to come into existence. Then the problems you encounter are not about getting rid of what you don't want, but about clearing the obstacles to create what you do want.

The question then becomes: What life story would you create to change your life if you changed the focus from solving problems to creating what you love?

Chapter 33

How Long Does It Take?

Groundhog Day in Punxsutawney, Pennsylvania on the second of February each year is a holiday created by a story:

> Legend has it that if Punxsutawney Phil emerges from his temporary burrow—a simulated tree stump at the rural site of Gobbler's Knob—on February 2 and sees his shadow, winter weather will continue for six more weeks across the United States. But if Phil doesn't see his shadow, then spring temperatures are just around the corner (Groundhog Day).

The story of Punxsutawney Phil is interesting enough as folklore, demonstrating the power of stories to create traditions. It also demonstrates the curious human habit of using animals of all varieties as sources of wisdom, in the form of morality tales to teach people some sort of lesson. In this case, a groundhog—also known as a woodchuck— has the ability to forecast how long winter will last.

The Elixir of Life for a Very Old Groundhog

What's especially interesting about Punxsutawney Phil is that he's a very old groundhog. In contrast to the typical ten-year lifespan of other merely mortal groundhogs, Punxsutawney Phil has been forecasting the weather for a long, long time:

> In 1887 a group of groundhog hunters from Punxsutawney dubbed themselves the Punxsutawney Groundhog Club and declared their furry oracle, Punxsutawney Phil, the one and only "official" weather-prognosticating groundhog. The Punxsutawney ceremony originated around the same time.
>
> ...
>
> According to Punxsutawney folklore, Phil owes his long lifespan to an "elixir of life," served every summer at the annual Groundhog Picnic, of which there are curiously no photographs" (Groundhog Day).

In the case of the Punxsutawney Groundhog Club, and the annual celebration of Groundhog Day at Gobbler's Knob, most people get the joke and understand that "Punxsutawney Phil" is a role to be cast each year rather than an extremely old woodchuck.

How Long Does It Take? 155

Can Punxsutawney Phil Change Your Life Story?

So what does the legendary groundhog Punxsutawney Phil have to do with changing your life by transforming your life story?

At the very least, Punxsutawney Phil inspired the brilliant movie, *Groundhog Day*, about an obnoxious, self-absorbed weatherman named Phil, played by Bill Murray. Phil is sent on assignment to cover Groundhog Day in Punxsutawney. Phil regards the whole experience as a colossal waste of his precious time and superior talent.

But through some sort of mysterious process, Phil is caught in a time loop, which forces him to relive Groundhog Day again and again. Whatever caused the loop to occur—which the movie makes no effort to explain—the experience gives Phil his own "elixir of life." Phil has the great gift of doing the day over and over again, until he finally gets it right.

Changing Pronouns to Be a Hero

In Phil's case, getting it right means changing pronouns from his self-absorbed first-person perspective. It's no longer all about Phil. Over countless repetitions of the day, Phil changes his perspective from what he wants for himself, to what he can do for others. His pronouns change from the self-focused *me, myself,* and *I* to the other-focused second and third person pronouns *you, he, she,* and *they.*

This change of pronouns is essential in the hero's journey. To be a hero, the hero-to-be has to broaden perspective, from the self-absorbed first person to include *you* and *he* and *she* and *they*. This change of pronouns also turns *I* into *us*. The hero always has a larger perspective than simply getting what the hero wants. The hero's journey must also benefit someone else.

Chapter 34

From Manipulation to Love

In *Groundhog Day*, self-centered Phil at first thinks only of himself. Even when he finds himself stuck in the time loop where he relives the same day again and again, he begins by using this experience in a very self-centered way.

His relationship with Rita, his producer, played by Andie MacDowell, demonstrates this self-centered focus. At the beginning of the story, Phil is very scornful about Rita and her cheerful enthusiasm.

When Phil realizes that he is stuck in a time loop, we watch him gather information from Nancy. He then uses this information to seduce Nancy. He even tells her that he loves her and has always loved her. It's all a lie, but he does get what he wants from Nancy.

As the story continues, Phil uses the same strategies in his attempts to seduce Rita.

Manipulation with a Twist

For example, he offers to buy Rita a drink. He orders "Jim Beam. Ice. Water" for himself. Then she orders "sweet vermouth on the rocks with a twist," which she says is her favorite drink.

When he relives the day, he again orders first. This time, he orders sweet vermouth on the rocks with a twist. She is impressed and tells him that it's her favorite drink.

There's nothing honest about any of Phil's efforts to impress Rita. It's all about manipulating her to get what he wants.

At this stage in the story, even when Phil is using the second person pronoun, *you*, he is stuck in the first-person pronoun stage of his transformation. It's still all about Phil and what Phil wants for himself.

Conditional Love in I-You Relationships

This is the inherent problem in any *I-you* relationship. In relationships between two people, it can be difficult to sort out genuine concern for the other with self-interest. Such relationships are often filled with conditional statements that begin with, "If you love me, you would…"

How much can you change your life if your relationships are filled with such "if you love me you will do what I want you to do" conditional love?

The Tiger Mother and the Violin

If you read the language of the "Tiger Mother" about parenting that created so much controversy—and generated so many book sales—you can see the same conditional language.

In the name of love and compassion, the Tiger Mother forces her children to do what she wants them to do, insisting that she does it only for the best interests of her children. Whether or not this method is effective parenting is not my focus here.

The most revealing words in the Time Magazine article, "The Roar of the Tiger Mom," are these words when Amy Chua describes her "epic battles" over her younger daughter's resistance to practice the violin:

> Finally, after a screaming, glass-smashing, very public showdown, the tiger mother admitted defeat: "Lulu," she said, "you win. It's over. We're giving up the violin (Paul, "Tiger Moms").

The words, *"we're* giving up the violin," get to the essence of my point here. Any relationship between two people—especially family relationships—is full of expectations and conditions. The barbed hook of such expectations is that they are so often expressed as selfless concern for the other. It's never that simple when it comes to *I-you* relationships.

In *Groundhog Day*, Phil gets past his manipulative self-absorption only when he experiences genuine concern and compassion for someone with no strings attached. This is the life changing power of love in the third person.

Chapter 35

Life Changing Unconditional Love

When we last left Phil, the weatherman stranded in Punxsutawney by a mysterious time loop was trying to get what he wanted in life by claiming that he loved Nancy and then Rita. At that point in Phil's life story, his talk about love was a tool of manipulation. Phil had not yet experienced unconditional love for Rita.

From False Declarations to Unconditional Love

The language of "love" is a profoundly tricky business, because it is so often shaped by our own needs and desires to get what we want. Love that is truly selfless, truly unconditional, truly focused on the other, is rare.

Phil undergoes his life changing transformation from an obnoxious, self-absorbed, miserable person when he experiences unconditional love for Rita.

It happens on the day that Phil tells the truth to Rita that he is stuck in a perpetual *Groundhog Day*, forced to live the same day again and again. She decides to wait with him through the rest of the day, to see what happens.

After she falls asleep, Phil speaks to Rita. His words are no longer false declarations of love. He has made the transition to genuine, unconditional love for her.

Meeting the Sleeping Goddess

In Joseph Campbell's, *The Hero with a Thousand Faces,* life changing events that transform the hero occur when the hero meets the *goddess.*

Campbell refers to "The Lady of the House of Sleep" in fairy tales and myth:

> She is the paragon of all paragons of beauty, the reply to all desire, the bliss-bestowing goal of every hero's earthly and unearthly quest. She is mother, sister, mistress, bride. Whatever in the world has lured, whatever has seemed to promise joy, has been premonitory of her existence—in the deep of sleep, if not in the cities and forests of the world. For she is the incarnation of the promise of perfection...(Campbell 110-111).

As Rita—the incarnation of the promise of perfection—sleeps, Phil experiences genuine, life transforming love for the first time in his life.

The Life Changing Power of Third-Person Love

Immediately after this transformative experience, Phil's capacity to love expands to include others, including the old, homeless man on the street.

Harold Ramis, the director and co-screenwriter of *Groundhog Day* says about Phil in "The Weight of Time" bonus feature on the *Groundhog Day* DVD:

> He stops worrying about himself all the time and then starts living a life of service to others. Then life gets very full and rich indeed. He embraces where he is and what he can do ("Weight of Time").

Phil's love and compassion for the old man is the first evidence of the life transforming effect of his unconditional love for Rita. This transforming change enables him to begin a life of service to others—the life changing power of love in the third person.

Conclusion

How to Get Out of the True Self Trap

We began by considering a favorite model of self-help work, the metaphor of Michelangelo's statue of David. As a metaphor, this model treats the Real You as a static entity trapped inside of you, obscured by your False Self. Getting rid of your False Self is the problem to be solved. The solution is to chip away at your False Self to reveal your True Self. The whole process is like mining for gold. You have to chip away at a lot of rock before you can find the lode of gold that is your True Self. It's a ridding process to solve the problem of your trapped and hidden True Self.

The second model of discovering your True Self is the hero's journey. It's also problem-oriented model. Unlike the statue of David model, it's focused outward. The source of the problem is an external threat rather than removing barriers to your True Self. Something or someone threatens the hero's wellbeing and the wellbeing of something that is important to the hero—whether family, friends, towns, cities, nations, planets, or something else that the hero loves. The solution to the problem is also a ridding process. The hero-to-be must do something to get rid of the threat. Doing something involves a journey from the familiar world of the hero-to-be to the dangerous world where the threat is located.

The heroes-to-be don't start out as heroes. Rather, they are ordinary people forced into some sort of journey because of external circumstances. The heroes accept the challenge, however reluctantly, and set out to get rid of the threat. They acquire enemies and allies along the way, and they also receive help and gifts for the journey from mentors. In the course of the journey, the heroes discover that they can do and be more than they realized.

As model of self discovery, the hero's journey is not about getting rid of your False Self to discover your True Self hidden away inside you. Rather, it's a model of discovering that you have capacities that you didn't know you had.

Limits of the Models

As models for living your life authentically and becoming your True Self, both models have limits. Both are problem-solving models about getting rid of what you don't want in your life.

The model of chipping away at your False Self is something like endlessly weeding your garden without planting what you want to grow and then wondering why you don't have any flowers growing in your garden.

A limitation of the hero's journey model is that it's a journey that was thrust upon you to get rid of what you don't want in your life.

Problem Solving or Creation?

Once again, I refer to Robert Fritz and his distinction between creating and problem solving. Problem solving is about getting rid of what you don't want. Creating is about bringing into existence what you do want. The difference between the two is love.

It's true that life is filled with problems. One problem after another. We all have problems to solve. The problems can range from the mundane to complicated, but underneath it all, a problem is something you don't want in your life. Solving a problem is about getting rid of what you don't want.

When you approach your life as a creator, you change focus from getting rid of what you don't want in your life to focus on creating what you do want in your life.

The Two Models as Creation Processes

Let's take another look at both metaphors from the perspective of creating what you do want in life.

Although the story about Michelangelo and his statue of David is a favorite self-help metaphor about chipping away at the False Self, it's more accurately a description of the creative process. Michelangelo loved the statue of David into existence. The stone he chipped away was not the problem to be solved. Rather his whole effort was focused on creating something because he truly wanted to create it. The result was Michelangelo's vision of David.

As a creation, Michelangelo's statue is certainly not an accurate representation of the "real David." According to the Bible, David was the second and greatest king of Israel. He created an empire and ruled for forty years. Most scholars set the dates for his reign around 1010-970 B.C.

Michelangelo was born in Caprese, Italy in 1475 A.D. and lived until 1564. This means that Michelangelo was born two thousand four hundred and forty-five years after David died.

An accurate model of the "real David" was not hidden in the block of marble. The model of David that emerged from the stone was the David of Michelangelo's imagination. Whatever the historical Semite called David looked like, it's fair to assume that he didn't bear much resemblance to the naked, clean-shaven, uncircumcised, Italian David who emerged from Michelangelo's block of marble.

Is the Idea of Your True Self a Trap?

When you attempt to become your True Self, what exactly are you doing? Are you discovering a True Self that is somehow hidden away within you? Are you discovering that your True Self is more than you imagined? Or are you discovering that the idea that you have a True Self trapped inside of you is itself a trap?

We started with the Platonic claim that there is an "ideal plane" where the Idea or Form of something exists in non-material form. Richard Tarnas claims that this single idea has shaped much Western thought.

A lot has happened since Plato. For one thing, we as human beings have discovered the mind-boggling reality of quantum physics. It all began when a few scientists at the beginning of the twentieth century discovered that atoms can be divided.

For a long time, humanity rested in the secure knowledge that atoms are the smallest indivisible particles in the universe. The word *atom* means *indivisible*, from the Greek *a* "not" and *tomos* "a cutting" from the verb *temnein* "to cut." In Latin, the word is *atomus* (*Online Etymology Dictionary*, "atom").

We humans knew that matter is made up of the indivisible atoms, with their electrons whizzing around the nucleus of each atom as little balls of matter.

Quantum physics upset that certainty. Suddenly, indivisible atoms became divisible. The foundation of matter itself became the ever-changing dance of energy. The fixed forms in the world we can observe became probabilities in the subatomic world we cannot see:

> Quantum physics is the study of the behavior of matter and energy at the molecular, atomic, nuclear, and even smaller microscopic levels. In the early 20th century, it was discovered that the laws that govern macroscopic objects do not function the same in such small realms (Jones, "quantum physics").

I still remember the day in an undergraduate physical chemistry course when the professor lectured about the "quantum leap." Although I don't remember much of what I learned about quantum mechanics a long time ago, I do remember that the professor said that the quantum leap is not about a particle of matter jumping from one energy level to another.

Rather, an election is energy. The "quantum leap" occurs when an atom with an electron on one energy level suddenly has an electron on a different level with no electron passing between the two levels. Particles of matter can't suddenly jump from here to there without somehow passing from one level to the other. This means that electrons are not matter. They are only energy.

In that moment, I had my first moment of awareness of the mysteries and wonders of quantum physics. I put down my pen and spent the rest of the class in a state of awe at the thought that the material world as we experience it is made up on the quantum level of nothing more than energy.

The unsettling realities of quantum physics demonstrate that the material world as we know it on the macro level is not so fixed on the quantum level. Marble stones in the material world are nothing more than energy on the quantum level. It's a dramatically different perception than Plato's claim that all we experience in the material world is based on a static Form or Idea of something in a non-material plane. From a quantum perspective, we live in a world of quantum potentials and probabilities rather than a world shaped by static patterns in an Ideal plane.

Quantum Physics and Your True Self

How does any of this apply to discovering, or becoming your True Self? I don't claim to have the answer to all of this, nor do I claim to understand much about quantum physics. However, quantum physics offers a perspective that goes beyond the idea that your True Self is already fixed and somehow trapped within you.

At the very least, quantum physics raises the question of whether you really have a True Self in some sort of static form to be discovered if you can only get rid of what hides it from you. Rather, quantum physics offers a vision of your self—whether it is "self" or "Self"—as a set possibilities. Possibilities means that you have the potential to make choices that define who you are—who you choose to be. You can create the life you love rather than focus on what you don't love. You can choose to see yourself as a creator rather than a problem to be solved.

It sets you free from the idea that you have to somehow rid yourself of all negative thoughts and feelings about yourself to have the life that you choose.

Changing Perspective

The greatest limitation of the David metaphor as it is typically used in self help work is that it's a first-person perspective. It's all about you:

> The first-person orientation is rampant in the human potential movement, where the focus is blatantly on self, sense of self, working on self, finding your own truth, being one with yourself, developing your self, reaching self-enlightenment, loving yourself, fulfilling yourself, and so on (Fritz, *Creating* 133).

Fritz advocates for a change in perspective from first person to third person to increase your ability to create what you choose in life.

> Another orientation that people can live in is the third person, as in language—he, she, him, her, it, they, them. In this orientation the focus is not on yourself, but rather outside yourself (Fritz, *Creating*, 136)

Changing the Metaphor about David

The story of Michelangelo and his statue of David can become a different metaphor by changing perspective from first person to third person. Michelangelo was not solving a problem in himself when he created his statue. He was loving something into existence.

That block of marble had limitless potential to turn into anything that the creator Michelangelo chose to create. He could have chipped away the stone and created an elephant. He could have made a statue of one of the gods and goddesses in the Roman Pantheon—Jupiter or Neptune or Diana or Venus. He could have made a statue of himself. He could have left the stone alone. There was no David hidden away in the stone, waiting to be revealed. Michelangelo's David emerged because Michelangelo chose to create it.

The life changing secret of Michelangelo's statue of David is that he chose to create it because he wanted it to exist. He wasn't looking in the mirror to fix some defect in himself.

Changing the Hero's Journey Story

What about hero's journey stories? What life changing secrets do these stories offer you? The essential secret of a hero's journey story is that you are capable of doing far more than you imagine. An even more significant secret is that you don't set out on a hero's journey to find your True Self.

In contrast to the first-person orientation of the David metaphor, the hero's journey model is a third-person perspective. A classic hero's journey story is about a reluctant hero who must do something difficult to save others from a threat. The hero is called to the journey. The hero doesn't choose it, and the hero is not on a quest to discover the hero's True Self by looking inward. Rather, heroes focus on saving others from the threat. In the process, heroes discover they are capable of doing more than they imagined, but self discovery was never the motivation of the journey.

The step beyond the hero's journey metaphor as a model for changing your life is that you don't have to wait for circumstances to compel you to take action against some threatening force. The deeper secret of the hero's journey model is that you can choose your journey. You can choose to be heroic, not because you must, but because you choose to be the hero in the service of a larger vision that is not just about what you want.

Robert Fritz emphasizes that creation involves a change in perspective, from the first person to the third person. It changes the focus from the endless quest to focus on finding your True Self to a vision of what you would love to create and those that your creation would serve.

Taking Action to Change Your Life

If you want to change your life, heroic stories reveal secrets about how to turn your attention away from fixing yourself, so that you can do something to create the life you desire to live. Without action, there is no story.

It's the difference between a photograph and a movie. Photographs are static. A photograph captures a moment in time. You can stare at a picture for hours on end, but nothing in that picture is going to change.

This is another reason why using Michelangelo's statue of David as a metaphor for discovering your True Self misses the essence of what it is to be a creator of what you love. Michelangelo's statue is a static object. David doesn't get off the pedestal and walk around. You are not a statue. As long as you're alive, your True Self cannot be captured in a photograph. Whatever potentials you have within you, whatever your doubts and failings and problems, "who you are" is not something static and frozen in time.

Rather, your life is a movie rather than a snapshot. The first movies were called "moving pictures" or "motion pictures" because that's what movies are. Each frame of film is a snapshot. A movie puts them together so that the pictures flow in a continuous motion, fast enough that your eyes cannot detect when one frame becomes another. It looks like one seamless flow.

The Futile Quest for Your True Self

The quest for your True Self is a something like searching for the pot of gold at the end of the rainbow. You'll never find it. However, when you change the focus of the metaphor from Michelangelo-as-the-rescuer-of-a-trapped David, into Michelangelo-the-creator-of-an-extraordinary-statue, you have a different perspective on who you are and who you can become. You can stop focusing on setting your "trapped True Self" free and focus on creating what you love, just because you love it.

The good news is that you don't have to be "perfect" to do it. You don't have to be "all put together." You don't have to solve all of your "issues." You can begin now to focus on what you would love to create rather on fixing what is "wrong" with you.

Similarly, the model of the hero's journey can be transformed from a call to an arduous journey to solve a problem into a model for living your life as a creator. You can choose the journey. In the process, you will discover that you have more capability than you ever imagined. The real secret is to put down the mirror and start your own self-chosen heroic journey as the creator of the life you choose to live.

I will give the last words to Robert Fritz:

> Creating is not designed to heal you, fix you, or satisfy you, but a way in which you can bring your talents, energies, actions, imagination, reason, intuition, and, yes, even love to the creation you desire (Fritz, *Creating* 20).

About the Author

Dr. Kalinda Rose Stevenson is an award-winning author, whose published writings include both academic and non-academic books.

She earned her Ph.D. at the Graduate Theological Union in Berkeley, California, in cooperation with the University of California at Berkeley.

She is a former teacher of university and theological seminary students. Most of all, she is a writer who loves to write.

She currently lives with her husband in the Las Vegas area of Nevada, where she writes books, tends to her sometimes neglected websites, works out in the gym, hikes in the desert with camera in hand, and stays out of casinos.

Find out more at:

KalindaRoseStevenson.com

TrueSelfTrap.com

BookWritingMadeSimple.com

DoesTheBibleReallySayThat.com

ABKAPublishing.com

Write a Review

If you like the book, please leave an honest review on Amazon. I welcome constructive feedback and would love to hear what you think of the book. I'm especially eager to hear how the book gave you insights about how to create the life you choose.

Writing a book is always a journey of discovery for me. It's one reason why I love to write. It's also the reason why no book is ever easy for me. Each book gives me insights, raises questions, challenges my own assumptions, and urges me to write another book.

I have barely scratched the surface of the difference that changing stories and changing perspective can make in how to live a life that is happy, productive, successful, and creative.

I intend to write additional books in "Heroic Stories to Change Your Life Series." Meanwhile, I plan to develop my website TrueSelfTrap.com and my Facebook page True Self Trap. I welcome your feedback, questions, insights, suggestions, and participation on the journey.

References

Free Bonus

Is Your True Self Meant to Be An Ant or a Mockingbird? Assumptions in Traditional Christian Religion and New Age Spirituality about Your True Self.

Go to TrueSelfTrap.com/antormockingbirdbonus

Sign up for your free downloadable PDF version now.

Anchor Bible Dictionary, s.v. "David."

"archetype." Online Etymology.

> http://www.etymonline.com/index.php?allowed_in_frame=0&search=archetype&searchmode=none (accessed June 26, 2014).

"atom." Online Etymology.

> http://www.etymonline.com/index.php?term=atom&allowed_in_frame=0 (accessed June 26, 2014).

"authentic." Online Etymology.

> http://www.etymonline.com/index.php?allowed_in_frame=0&search=authentic&searchmode=none (accessed June 26, 2014).

"authority." Online Etymology.

> http://www.etymonline.com/index.php?allowed_in_frame=0&search=authority&searchmode=none (accessed June 26, 2014).

"Be Prepared." US Scouting Service Project.

> http://usscouts.org/advance/boyscout/bsmotto.asp (accessed June 26, 2014).

Billingsley, Peter, et al. *A Christmas Story*. DVD. Directed by Bob Clark. Burbank, CA: Warner Home Video, 1999.

Bonnet, James. *Stealing Fire from the Gods: The Complete Guide to Story for Writers and Filmmakers*. 2d ed. Studio City, CA: Michael Wise Productions, 2006.

Burns, Frank. "The Novocaine Mutiny." *M*A*S*H*. DVD. Directed by Harry Morgan. Beverly Hills, CA: Twentieth Century Fox Home Entertainment, 2003.

Campbell, Joseph. *The Hero With A Thousand Faces*. 2nd ed. Bollingen Series XVII. Princeton, New Jersey: Princeton University Press, 1968.

Donne, John. "For whom the bell tolls." Famous Poetry Online. http://www.famousliteraryworks.com/donne_for_whom_the_bell_tolls.htm (accessed June 26, 2014).

"focus." Dictionary.com. http://dictionary.reference.com/browse/focus. (accessed June 26, 2014).

Fritz, Robert. *Creating*. New York: Fawcett Columbine, 1991.

Fritz, Robert. *The Path of Least Resistance: Learning to Become the Creative Force in Your Own Life*. Revised Edition. New York: Fawcett Columbine, 1989.

Hanks, Tom, et al. *Apollo 13*. DVD. Directed by Ron Howard. Universal City, CA: Universal Home Video, 1998.

Hanks, Tom, and Meg Ryan. *Joe Versus the Volcano*. DVD. Directed by John Patrick Shanley. Burbank, CA: Warner Home Video, 2002.

Hill, Napoleon. *Think and Grow Rich Action Pack*. New York: Plume Books, 1988.

Lennon, John. "Beautiful Boy." AZLyrics. http://www.azlyrics.com/lyrics/johnlennon/beautifulboydarlingboy.html (accessed June 26, 2014).

Murray, Bill, and Andie MacDowell. *Groundhog Day*. DVD. Directed by Harold Ramis. Culver City, CA: Columbia TriStar Home Entertainment, 2002.

Paul, Annie Murphy. "Tiger Moms: Is Tough Parenting Really the Answer?" Time, January 2011. http://content.time.com/time/magazine/article/0,9171,2043477,00.html (accessed June 26, 2014).

Ryan, James. *Screenwriting from the Heart: The Technique of the Character-Driven Screenplay*. New York: Billboard Books, 2000.

"story." Online Etymology. http://www.etymonline.com/index.php?allowed_in_frame=0&search=story&searchmode=none (accessed June 26, 2014).

Tarnas, Richard. *The Passion of the Western Mind: Understanding the Ideas That Have Shaped Our World View*. New York: Harmony Books, 1991.

Wood, Elijah, et al. *Lord of the Rings: The Fellowship of the Ring*. DVD. New Line Home Entertainment, 2002.

Index

A

accomplish, 1, 12, 68, 69, 80, 84, 87, 89, 118, 121, 144
action, 147, 149, 173, 174
actions, 13, 56, 74, 176
addictions, 80
adult, 50, 59, 62, 66, 79
adults, 55, 56, 62, 78, 79
adversary, 52, 53, 54, 143
afraid, 76, 93, 103, 109, 110, 111, 112, 113
air rifle, 49, 50, 55, 56, 61, 65, 67, 68
alive, 55, 126, 174
allies, 164
alone, 80, 87, 88, 89, 130, 172
amazement, 84
Apollo 13, 122, 125, 127, 128, 129, 132, 133, 134, 137, 138, 182
archetypal, 3, 6, 40
archetype, 3, 40, 181
archetypes, 4, 40
ascents and descents, 117, 118
assessment, 138
assumption, 7
astronaut, 125, 133
astronauts, 125, 126, 127, 129, 133
atoms, 167, 168
authentic, 15, 16, 17, 19, 20, 21, 22, 23, 68, 101, 102, 103, 104, 106, 107, 109, 111, 113, 181
authentically, 20, 23, 164
authority, 15, 19, 20, 21, 22, 23, 181
awareness, 62, 101, 102, 103, 147, 169

B

Banks, Joe, 77, 78, 80, 83, 93, 94, 97, 99, 101, 102, 103, 104, 105, 106, 107, 108, 109, 110, 111, 112, 113, 182

barriers, 163
BB gun, 55, 68
Be Prepared, 44, 181
beach, 74, 75
Beautiful Boy, 43, 182
beauty, 82, 160
becoming, vi, 4, 109, 113, 164, 170
belief, vi, 3, 16, 19, 59
benefit, 85, 129, 131, 154
betrayal, 59, 61, 62, 63, 143
betrayed, 61, 62, 98
Bonnet, James, 45, 57, 117
boobaroo, 94, 99, 106, 111
Boy Scout motto, 44
boys, 50, 67, 68
brain cloud, 102, 105, 106
bullies, 51, 54, 56
bully, 50, 51, 52, 53, 55

C

call, 3, 28, 35, 45, 57, 175
called, 3, 40, 62, 94, 98, 121, 133, 166, 174
Campbell, Joseph, 40, 53, 65, 67, 87, 160, 182
capable, xii, 7, 8, 15, 68, 172, 173
capacities, 15, 164
capacity, 76, 144, 161
capitalization, 3
capitalized, 2
catastrophe, 126, 130
celebrities, 129
certainty, 168
challenge, 36, 37, 44, 45, 57, 62, 68, 78, 121, 131, 143, 144, 164
change, 3, xi, 2, 7, 12, 13, 14, 19, 20, 27, 28, 29, 31, 33, 41, 43, 46, 49, 54, 63, 67, 68, 74, 76, 80, 87, 89, 101, 103, 104, 109, 117, 119, 120, 123, 124, 128, 138, 141, 142, 144, 145, 147, 150, 154, 156, 161, 165, 171, 173, 174, 175

changeless, 2, 3, 4, 6
changing, 7, 20, 23, 28, 32, 35, 36, 38, 40, 45, 46, 73, 106, 113, 142, 147, 153, 158, 159, 160, 161, 168, 171, 172, 173, 179
character, 3, 7, 23, 101, 105
characteristic, 52
characters, 3, 7, 66, 103, 142, 143, 144
child, 50, 60, 61, 65, 68, 69, 79, 143
childhood, 54, 62, 66, 68, 78, 94
children, 50, 51, 53, 56, 57, 59, 62, 66, 67, 68, 78, 157
chip away, 2, 7, 163
chipping away, 2, 6, 7, 8, 165, 166
choice, 46
choices, 23, 35, 95, 106, 108, 142, 170
choose, xii, 8, 23, 110, 138, 141, 142, 147, 170, 171, 173, 176, 179
Christian church, 79
Christmas, 49, 51, 55, 65, 66, 67, 68
Christmas Story, A, 49, 51, 54, 55, 59, 61, 65, 66, 182
Chua, Amy, 157
circles, 117, 118, 119, 120, 122, 123, 124
clean thinking
  get your thinking clean, 7
collaboration, 85
companion, 89, 102
companions, 87, 88
competition, 85
computer, 132
concern, 125, 127, 156, 158
conditional, 156, 157
connected, 28, 85, 126, 127, 129, 130, 131
connection, 20, 57, 85, 102
courage, 111, 112
create, 20, 41, 80, 97, 138, 142, 144, 148, 150, 151, 166, 170, 171, 172, 173, 174, 175, 179
creation, 147, 165, 166, 173, 176
creative process, 143, 166
creator, 165, 170, 172, 174, 175
current reality, 131, 138
currently, 138, 177
cycles, 117, 119, 121
cynical, 73

D

dangerous, 56, 57, 164
dark side of the moon, 126, 129, 130
David, 1, 2, 3, 6, 52, 53, 163, 166, 171, 172, 174, 175, 181
dead, 93, 134, 138
decide, 16, 41, 149
decision, 41, 45, 106, 112, 137, 138
decoder pin, 59, 60, 61
defeat, 135, 136, 137, 138, 157
define, 16, 144, 150, 170
defining, 4, 43, 44, 52
description, 85, 166
desire, 1, 2, 40, 41, 55, 59, 120, 127, 148, 160, 174, 176
die, 19, 76, 77, 94, 95, 98, 106, 107, 112, 113, 130
difference, xii, 7, 19, 21, 22, 23, 68, 87, 97, 138, 147, 148, 165, 174, 179
disbelief, 61
discovering, 7, 8, 20, 143, 163, 164, 167, 170, 174
divisible, 168
do, vi, xii, 1, 2, 3, 8, 13, 14, 15, 16, 19, 27, 31, 32, 35, 36, 37, 41, 44, 46, 56, 57, 59, 62, 65, 66, 67, 68, 69, 73, 74, 75, 76, 78, 80, 82, 83, 88, 89, 93, 94, 95, 103, 107, 108, 109, 110, 112, 119, 124, 137, 138, 141, 142, 144, 147, 148, 149, 150, 151, 153, 154, 156, 157, 161, 164, 165, 166, 168, 170, 172, 173, 174, 175
dollars, 36, 37, 38, 40, 41, 94, 99, 102, 103, 107, 135, 136
Donne, John, 127
Dr. Ellison, 105, 106, 107, 109, 110
dream, 2, 51, 55, 56, 57, 67, 68, 133, 134, 138
dream smashers, 55, 56
dreams, 1, 12, 56, 57, 59, 65, 66, 67, 68, 69, 84, 87, 138

E

Easter Bunny, 62
election, 169
emotions, 11, 39, 40, 41

Index   189

enemies, 164
energy, 148, 168, 169
epigraph, 7
Esau, 97, 98
essence, 7, 28, 39, 68, 76, 125, 127, 157, 174
essential, 44, 105, 106, 113, 154, 172
ethical, 36, 38, 41
event, 27, 28, 31, 32, 35, 39, 40, 43, 44, 45, 73, 141, 142
events, 28, 29, 38, 74, 125, 141, 142, 143, 144, 148, 160
exists, 2, 5, 138, 167
experience, 5, 7, 27, 28, 39, 43, 44, 45, 56, 59, 61, 84, 104, 117, 153, 155, 161, 169
external, 22, 163, 164

F

failure, 0, 133, 135, 136
False Self, 1, 2, 7, 163, 164, 165, 166
father, 66, 84, 98, 101, 103
finest hour, 126
fireman, 110
first person, 153, 154, 156, 171, 172, 173
flat tire, 25, 27, 28, 29, 31, 32, 35, 37, 38, 39, 40, 43, 44, 45, 73, 141, 142, 144, 148
flaw, 105, 142
focus, xi, xii, 13, 118, 121, 124, 131, 150, 155, 157, 165, 170, 171, 173, 175, 182
form, 2, 3, 5, 53, 78, 88, 102, 151, 167, 170
Form, 4, 5, 167, 169
free, 2, 7, 19, 22, 23, 104, 170, 175, 181
freedom, 69, 131, 145, 150
friends, 16, 50, 87, 88, 163
Fritz, Robert, 138, 147, 165, 173, 176
Frodo, 88, 118
future, 130

G

gift, 66, 68, 105, 106, 107, 153
gifts, 164
goal, 122, 134, 160

goals, 1, 4, 12, 16, 121
God, 38
good news, 119
good will, 127, 129
Greek, 3, 4, 19, 21, 22, 40, 167
Greek philosophy, 4
Groundhog Day, 151, 152, 153, 155, 158, 159, 161, 183
grownup, 69

H

Hanks, Tom, 93, 125, 132, 133
Harry Potter, 65
hate, 37, 39, 41, 148, 150
health, 93, 99, 102, 103, 143
help, 1, 4, 6, 14, 28, 37, 38, 60, 80, 88, 89, 125, 128, 129, 131, 132, 163, 164, 166
helpless, 79
helps, 130
hero, 40, 44, 45, 46, 49, 50, 51, 52, 53, 54, 55, 56, 57, 65, 67, 74, 77, 78, 79, 80, 85, 87, 88, 89, 95, 99, 102, 103, 104, 105, 106, 107, 109, 110, 111, 113, 118, 141, 142, 143, 144, 147, 148, 149, 153, 154, 160, 163, 164, 165, 172, 173, 175, 182
Hero with a Thousand Faces, The, 53, 160
heroes, 45, 50, 52, 54, 57, 75, 76, 78, 79, 148, 164, 173
heroes-to-be, 164
heroic, 7, 40, 46, 51, 53, 55, 57, 59, 63, 66, 67, 68, 73, 74, 75, 76, 80, 85, 88, 89, 106, 110, 141, 150, 173
hero-to-be, 154, 164
hidden, 3, 6, 7, 163, 164, 166, 167, 172
hierarchy of needs, 85
Hill, Napoleon, 135, 137
home, 53, 94, 125, 126, 127, 128, 129, 131, 132, 134
honeysuckle, 82, 83, 84
honor and money, 97
hope, 11, 78, 79, 80, 127, 130
Howard, Ron, 126, 182
human, 20, 39, 41, 74, 77, 106, 117, 118, 126, 127, 129, 132, 144, 151, 167, 171

humanity, 39, 126, 167

I

idea, xii, 2, 5, 6, 40, 67, 85, 107, 108, 111, 136, 147, 167, 170
Idea, 4, 5, 6, 167, 169
ideal plane, 5, 167
Ideal plane, 6, 170
imagine, xii, 5, 8, 37, 137, 172
imagined, 8, 15, 35, 167, 173, 176
impossible, 126, 134, 137
indivisible, 167, 168
inertia, 149
inherited, 15, 16, 19, 20
I-you relationship, 156, 158

J

Jesus, 0, 79, 98
Joe Versus the Volcano, 77, 83, 93, 97, 99, 101, 105, 107, 108, 109, 112, 113, 182
journey, 40, 44, 45, 46, 51, 52, 53, 63, 65, 67, 80, 85, 87, 88, 89, 102, 103, 104, 105, 106, 107, 109, 113, 118, 141, 142, 143, 144, 147, 148, 149, 150, 154, 163, 164, 165, 172, 173, 175, 179
journeys, 149
jump, 77, 94, 106, 107, 111, 112, 169
Jung, Carl, 40

K

know, 20, 23, 38, 41, 59, 61, 62, 66, 77, 82, 83, 84, 94, 100, 110, 111, 119, 123, 125, 128, 138, 143, 164, 169
know yourself, 20
knowing, 20, 21, 41, 67, 123

L

leaps of faith, 112
Lennon, John, 43
lie, 75, 94, 105, 106, 149, 155
life, v, 0, 1, xi, xii, 1, 2, 6, 8, 11, 12, 13, 14, 15, 16, 19, 20, 21, 22, 23, 27, 28, 29, 31, 32, 33, 35, 36, 38, 40, 41, 43, 45, 46, 49, 54, 56, 57, 62, 63, 65, 66, 68, 71, 74, 75, 76, 77, 78, 80, 81, 84, 85, 87, 89, 91, 93, 94, 95, 97, 99, 101, 103, 104, 106, 107, 108, 109, 115, 117, 118, 119, 121, 123, 124, 128, 129, 131, 132, 135, 136, 137, 139, 141, 142, 143, 144, 145, 147, 148, 149, 150, 152, 153, 156, 158, 159, 160, 161, 164, 165, 166, 170, 171, 172, 173, 174, 175, 179, 182
limitation, 165, 171
limits, 164
linear objective, 122
Little Orphan Annie, 59, 60, 61
live, xii, 1, 2, 6, 8, 13, 16, 17, 19, 20, 21, 23, 44, 84, 87, 94, 103, 106, 107, 108, 118, 119, 127, 130, 159, 169, 171, 174, 179
live it well, 107
lives, 16, 23, 31, 32, 66, 67, 73, 76, 78, 84, 89, 93, 100, 118, 119, 121, 129, 131, 143, 177
location, xi, 21, 22, 122
lonely, 87, 130, 132
Lord of the Rings, The, 88, 118
love, 39, 83, 108, 113, 144, 148, 150, 155, 156, 157, 158, 159, 160, 161, 165, 170, 173, 174, 175, 176, 179
Lovell, Jim, 125, 132, 133

M

M*A*S*H, 22, 182
MacDowell, Andie, 155, 183
manipulation, 155, 159
manipulative, 158
mantra, 78
marble, 166, 169, 172
Maslow, Abraham, 85, 87
material world, 5, 6, 169
matter, 2, 23, 81, 108, 135, 138, 168, 169
men, 67, 68, 125, 126, 127, 129, 133, 136
mentor, 102, 105
mentors, 87, 88, 164
message, 60, 61

metaphor, 1, 2, 4, 6, 31, 163, 166, 171, 172, 173, 174, 175
metaphorical, 32, 39, 44, 45, 129
metaphysical, 131
method, 141, 157
Michelangelo, 1, 2, 3, 6, 163, 166, 171, 172, 174, 175
miracle, 132
mirror, 172
model, xii, 1, 8, 67, 85, 87, 89, 117, 118, 141, 142, 148, 163, 164, 165, 166, 172, 173, 175
money, 11, 36, 37, 38, 41, 68, 75, 93, 94, 95, 97, 99, 101, 103, 104, 105, 112, 135, 148
Moon, 122, 123, 129, 133, 134, 138
moon mission, 123, 124, 133
morality tales, 151
mortality, 106
mother, 53, 56, 66, 157, 160
movie, 32, 59, 77, 93, 95, 100, 103, 108, 122, 125, 129, 149, 153, 174
movies, 46, 49, 77, 80, 174
Mr. Granamore, 94, 99, 105, 106, 110, 111
Murray, Bill, 153

N

NASA, 122, 123, 126
need, 4, 6, 32, 37, 41, 46, 59, 69, 74, 75, 78, 80, 84, 108, 112, 121, 124, 128, 138, 145, 149
New Year, 11, 13
non-material, 5, 6, 167, 169

O

obedience, 15, 22, 23, 24
obstacle, 4, 78
obstacles, vi, 142, 143, 150
occurrence, 31, 32, 45
Old Man, 66
ordinariness, 67
ordinary, 27, 31, 32, 65, 66, 68, 75, 103, 141, 164
Ovaltine, 59, 60, 61

P

paradox, 87, 88, 106
paradoxical, 105
parents, 62, 66
particles, 167
path, 24, 62, 126, 137
Path of Least Resistance, The, 138, 147, 182
patriarchal, 98
Patricia, 83, 101, 102, 103, 104, 113
people, 23, 32, 39, 40, 52, 55, 59, 66, 75, 77, 78, 82, 83, 84, 88, 93, 95, 97, 99, 100, 103, 108, 111, 112, 125, 126, 127, 129, 130, 131, 132, 134, 138, 151, 152, 156, 157, 164, 171
perfect, 3, 7, 143, 175
perfection, 160
permanent, 5, 6, 138, 141
persevere, 76, 143
persistence, 135
personal names, 2
perspective, 6, 7, 28, 53, 112, 131, 137, 153, 154, 166, 169, 170, 171, 173, 175, 179
photograph, 174
planes, 5
Plato, 4, 5, 6, 167, 169
Platonic, 6, 167
possibilities, 170
possible, 23, 37, 87, 122, 123, 131, 144
potential, 35, 41, 109, 170, 171, 172
potentials, 170, 174
power, xi, 11, 12, 13, 17, 22, 27, 68, 79, 88, 118, 125, 128, 141, 151, 158, 161
prayers, 38
preparation, 46
prepared, 44
price tag, 97, 99, 100
priceless, 94, 97, 99, 100, 101, 102, 103, 104
probabilities, 168, 170
problem, xii, 7, 11, 22, 68, 73, 74, 75, 76, 77, 78, 79, 80, 88, 109, 137, 141, 142, 143, 147, 148, 149, 156, 163, 164, 165, 166, 170, 172, 175
problem solving, xii, 147, 148, 165

problems, 32, 45, 57, 74, 75, 76, 77, 80, 84, 102, 126, 129, 130, 132, 141, 148, 149, 150, 165, 174
process, 7, 19, 20, 21, 22, 23, 46, 142, 144, 153, 163, 173, 176
profanity, 52, 66
pronouns, 153, 154
Punxsutawney Phil, 151, 152, 153
purpose, 3, 6, 97, 117, 144
pyramid, 87, 88

Q

quantum, 167, 168, 169, 170
quest, xii, 6, 7, 61, 87, 160, 173, 175, 179
question, 3, 4, 12, 13, 20, 22, 51, 67, 80, 87, 107, 111, 134, 135, 138, 150, 170
questions, vi, xii, 1, 6, 13, 38, 95, 108, 179
quit, 134, 135, 136, 137, 138
quitting, 135, 136, 137

R

rainbows, 81, 82, 83, 84
Ralphie, 49, 50, 51, 52, 53, 55, 56, 59, 60, 61, 65, 66, 67, 68
Ramis, Harold, 161, 183
reaction, 28
ready, 43, 44, 45, 46
Real You, 7, 163
reality, 5, 44, 62, 167
Red Ryder, 49, 51, 55, 56, 61, 66, 67, 68
reframing, 73, 76
refusal, 57
refuse, 45, 57
relationships, 11, 156, 157
reluctant, 149, 173
rescue from without, 53
rescued, 53
response, 28, 73, 82
responses, 29
rid, xii, 2, 7, 148, 150, 163, 164, 165, 170
ridding process, 2, 163, 164
risk, 57
rock, 35, 163

rule, 12, 13, 15, 16, 22
rules, 11, 12, 23
ruthless, 142, 143
ruthlessness, 144
Ryan, James, 3, 7
Ryan, Meg, 101, 103, 182

S

salvation, 51, 54, 78, 80
Santa Claus, 56, 61, 62
save, 46, 49, 52, 53, 54, 55, 59, 77, 78, 79, 80, 111, 112, 173
saves, 49, 51
savior, 51, 53, 54, 77, 78, 79, 86, 106
saviors, 67, 79
screenwriting, 142
secret, 1, 59, 60, 61, 172, 173
secrets, 172, 174
self, vi, xi, 2, 3, 7, 16, 22, 23, 85, 86, 87, 88, 89, 99, 101, 102, 103, 107, 109, 111, 113, 153, 154, 155, 156, 158, 159, 163, 164, 166, 170, 171, 173
self discovery, 164, 173
self help, 1, 2, 7, 171
self-actualized, 85, 86, 87, 88
self-awareness, 23, 101, 103
self-interest, 156
self-made men, 87
separation, 85, 131
service, 35, 161, 173
should, 2
simple
    make it simple, 7
sleep, 125, 160
sleeping goddess, 160
smashed, 56
solitary, 85
solution, 4, 7, 45, 57, 102, 163
solve, 74, 75, 76, 88, 130, 141, 143, 149, 163, 165, 175
solving, 73, 74, 75, 147, 150, 164, 165, 171
soul, 93, 94, 101, 102, 103, 104, 105, 107
soul sick, 101, 102, 103, 104, 107
spinning plates, 119
static, 163, 169, 170, 174

statue, 1, 2, 3, 163, 166, 171, 172, 174, 175
statues, 3
Stealing Fire from the Gods, 45, 57, 117, 182
stone, 2, 3, 6, 166, 172
stories, v, 1, xi, xii, 6, 7, 8, 9, 11, 12, 13, 14, 15, 16, 19, 20, 21, 22, 23, 25, 27, 28, 38, 39, 40, 45, 46, 47, 51, 52, 53, 57, 62, 63, 65, 66, 67, 68, 71, 73, 74, 75, 76, 79, 81, 87, 91, 93, 97, 98, 115, 117, 118, 123, 139, 141, 142, 143, 145, 147, 148, 151, 172, 174, 179
story, 0, 3, 1, 6, 7, 12, 14, 19, 20, 27, 28, 29, 32, 33, 35, 36, 39, 40, 45, 49, 51, 52, 53, 54, 67, 68, 73, 74, 76, 77, 78, 93, 97, 99, 101, 102, 104, 105, 106, 108, 110, 112, 117, 118, 119, 121, 122, 123, 124, 125, 126, 128, 129, 133, 135, 136, 137, 141, 142, 144, 145, 147, 148, 150, 151, 153, 155, 156, 159, 166, 171, 172, 173, 174, 182, 183
storyteller, 12, 141, 142, 143, 144, 145, 147, 149, 150
storywheel, 117, 118, 119, 121
storywheels, 118, 119, 121
straight lines, 121, 123
stuck, 0, 12, 16, 19, 20, 45, 57, 66, 67, 103, 120, 155, 156, 159
success, 14, 85, 87, 88, 89, 134, 135, 136, 137
successful, 1, 4, 6, 85, 86, 133, 136, 179

T

Tarnas, Richard, 3, 4, 6, 167, 183
tells, 12, 13, 15, 20, 27, 29, 36, 56, 63, 74, 89, 112, 135, 138, 145, 147
template, 5
temporary, 135, 137, 138, 151
theme, 56
Think and Grow Rich, 135, 182
thinking, 3, 4, 134, 137
third person, 154, 158, 161, 171, 172, 173
thoughts, 19, 170

threat, 73, 74, 76, 77, 105, 163, 164, 173
threatening, 75, 173
threats, 75
Tiger Mother, 157
time, 11, 13, 19, 22, 32, 39, 43, 55, 66, 82, 94, 103, 106, 107, 108, 110, 118, 121, 130, 133, 144, 148, 152, 153, 155, 156, 157, 159, 160, 161, 167, 168, 174, 183
time loop, 153, 155, 159
toadies, 51, 56
toady, 50, 53
Tooth Fairy, 62
traded, 97, 103, 107
tradeoffs, 99, 100, 105
traditional, vi, 15, 16, 19
transform, 14, 21, 46, 65, 141, 144, 160
transformation, 19, 65, 144, 156, 159
transforming, 20, 21, 22, 40, 46, 63, 124, 142, 145, 153, 160, 161
trap, 167
trapped, 2, 3, 6, 7, 126, 163, 167, 170, 175
true self, 0, vi, xi, xii, 2, 3, 6, 7, 101, 111, 163, 164, 167, 170, 172, 173, 174, 175, 179, 181
trust, 39, 59, 60, 61, 62
truth, 29, 54, 62, 63, 74, 75, 83, 89, 104, 105, 106, 107, 110, 113, 118, 128, 132, 145, 159, 171
truth teller, 105, 106

U

unchanging, 5
unconditional, 159, 160, 161
unexpected, 28, 29, 31, 43, 141, 143
universal, 39, 41, 68, 74, 78
unwilling, 103, 108, 134
urgency, 43
urgent, 43, 45, 60, 73, 76, 141, 148, 149

V

value, 80, 103, 118
victim, 50, 52, 53, 54
victims, 50, 51, 53, 54, 56

visible, 5, 125
vision, vi, 4, 55, 63, 85, 111, 117, 127, 166, 170, 173
volcano, 77, 94, 106, 107, 111, 112

W

wallet, 36, 37, 38, 40, 41
Waponi, 77, 102, 106, 107, 113
Waponi Woo, 77, 102, 106, 107, 113
warning, 55, 56, 57, 60
wasted, 107
Weight of Time, 161
wellbeing, 163
who, 7, 11, 12, 13, 20, 21, 23, 29, 32, 37, 40, 41, 47, 49, 50, 51, 53, 55, 57, 59, 60, 61, 62, 65, 66, 67, 68, 77, 78, 79, 83, 87, 89, 97, 98, 99, 101, 103, 104, 109, 111, 113, 121, 129, 130, 131, 133, 134, 135, 141, 142, 144, 145, 167, 170, 173, 174, 175, 177
wisdom, 15, 62, 107, 108, 151
women, 67, 103
wonder, 83, 84, 134
world, vi, 4, 5, 11, 12, 23, 45, 50, 51, 53, 56, 57, 59, 61, 62, 66, 75, 78, 79, 82, 84, 85, 103, 122, 124, 126, 127, 130, 132, 141, 160, 164, 168, 169
worldview, 3
worthy, 60

Y

you, 2, vi, xii, 1, 2, 4, 5, 6, 7, 8, 12, 13, 14, 15, 16, 19, 20, 21, 22, 23, 27, 28, 29, 31, 32, 35, 36, 37, 38, 39, 40, 41, 43, 44, 45, 46, 49, 54, 57, 59, 60, 62, 68, 69, 73, 74, 75, 76, 78, 79, 80, 84, 87, 89, 93, 97, 98, 99, 101, 104, 107, 108, 109, 110, 111, 112, 113, 119, 121, 123, 124, 125, 128, 129, 130, 131, 132, 137, 138, 141, 142, 143, 144, 145, 147, 148, 149, 150, 154, 156, 157, 163, 164, 165, 166, 167, 170, 171, 172, 173, 174, 175, 176, 179
you'll shoot your eye out, 55, 56, 57
yourself, 7, 12, 15, 16, 19, 20, 23, 29, 35, 36, 46, 54, 62, 74, 78, 79, 89, 113, 170, 171, 174

www.ingramcontent.com/pod-product-compliance
Lightning Source LLC
Chambersburg PA
CBHW061642040426
42446CB00010B/1532